by
Henrik Ibsen

New Adaptation by
**Kirsten Brandt and
Anne-Charlotte Hanes Harvey**

From a Platform Translation by
Anne-Charlotte Hanes Harvey

STEELE SPRING
STAGE RIGHTS

www.stagerights.com

For all stage performance inquiries, please contact:

Steele Spring Stage Rights
3845 Cazador Street
Los Angeles, CA 90065
(323) 739-0413
www.stagerights.com

Artwork by Jake Fruend

WORLD PREMIERE BILLING
A DOLL'S HOUSE
By Henrik Ibsen

New Adaptation by
Kirsten Brandt and Anne-Charlotte Hanes Harvey
From a Platform Translation by Anne-Charlotte Hanes Harvey

World Premiere at the Old Globe Theatre
San Diego, California

Barry Edelstein   Michael G. Murphy
Artistic Director   Managing Director

March 23 – April 21, 2013
Sheryl and Harvey White Theatre
Conrad Prebys Theatre Center

Directed by Kirsten Brandt
Scenic Design by Sean Fanning
Costume Design by Alina Bokovikova
Lighting Design by David Lee Cuthbert
Sound Design by Paul Peterson
Casting by Caparelliotis Casting
Stage Manager, Jess Slocum

Cast (in order of appearance)

Helene .... Katie Whalley
Nora Helmer .... Gretchen Hall
Torvald Helmer .... Fred Arsenault
Mrs. Kristine Linde .... Nisi Sturgis
Nils Krogstad/Porter .... Richard Baird
Dr. Rank... Jack Koenig
Anne-Marie .... Amanda Naughton

CHARACTER DESCRIPTIONS

Minimum Casting Requirements: 4F, 3M

NORA HELMER, 29, married to Torvald and mother of three. On the surface, she appears to be playful and naïve but underneath is intelligent and resourceful. She is a major force waiting to be born.

TORVALD HELMER, early 40s, a lawyer, Nora's husband, just appointed Bank Director, obsessed with his new status and his place in society.

DOCTOR RANK, M.D., 40-50, bachelor and close friend of the Helmers, harbors affection for Nora. He is ill and knows he is dying.

KRISTINE LINDE, early 30s, childhood friend of Nora's, down to earth and practical, widowed 3 years ago and is in need of employment.

NILS KROGSTAD, early 40s, a widower and a trial lawyer with a soiled reputation, he knows Nora's secret and will use it to his advantage if he has no other choice.

ANNE-MARIE, 50s but feels much older, originally Nora's wet-nurse, now the nanny to the Helmer's children, devoted and opinionated.

HELENE, early 20s, the Helmers' maid, helpful and quick on her feet, but really would rather be someplace else.

PORTER, a delivery boy, can be doubled with Krogstad.

RUN TIME

2 hours, 10 minutes (one intermission)

AUTHORS' NOTES

This adaptation of *A Doll's House* makes Ibsen's intentions more accessible to a contemporary American English-speaking director and cast through a slimmed down text that can be performed in any theatrical space.

We boldly remove one important feature of the original, the Helmers' three children. Although they are not *seen* on stage, they are nevertheless very *present* in the show: they are talked about, there is traffic in and out of the nursery, their toys and articles of clothing are strewn about and picked up, and their voices are heard from off stage.

There are four other aspects of this *A Doll's House* adaptation that aim specifically to bring Ibsen's original to the minds of the creative team. One: Translation from Dano-Norwegian into English normally results in 15-25% lengthening, a death knell for spoken dialogue. Here, we maintain Ibsen's forward momentum by deliberately slimming down— not simplifying— the text. Two: Major insight into characters and action is offered by clearly showing Ibsen's distinction between formal and informal address. This is accomplished by spelling "you"— the personal pronoun for second person singular and plural— with a capital letter for formal address and lower case for informal address. This dual spelling (You/you) gives director and actors subtle insight into the original as a blueprint for character relationships and interaction. Three: Ibsen's delicate gradation of social distancing is indicated also by the characters' use of first names, which informs blocking, personal space, activities, power relationships, and more. Four: Ibsen is a master of different voices, a fact which is often obscured by a translator's single voice. This adaptation captures the different speech patterns of Ibsen's characters and bring their varied voices to life.

The overall advantage of this adaptation is that it embraces the original while making it accessible to an American audience. Originally commissioned by the Old Globe and presented in the round, the script flexibly works in any type of performance venue: round, proscenium, thrust, etc. The script includes one notable directorial line change. In Ibsen's ending, Nora leaves, Torvald reacts to her leaving with a flicker of hope, and then Ibsen kills this hope by having Torvald hear Nora slamming the heavy door downstairs. In our adaptation, Torvald's realization of the finality of Nora's leaving is emphasized by moving the word "empty" to *follow* the door slam. The reason? Today's audience will not necessarily understand the layout of the building and the significance of the heavy door slam with which Ibsen ends the play. In our adaptation, the word "Empty!"— Torvald's reaction to the door slam— signals the end of the action and his hope.

ACT I

SCENE 1

A pleasant and tastefully, though not expensively, decorated living room. A door[i] leads out to the entry; another door leads in to Helmer's office.[ii] Between these doors a piano. A third door leads to the dining room and the Helmers' bedroom. In the opposite wall a fourth door, leading to the nursery, and a window. Close to the window a round table with easy chairs and a small sofa. On another wall, a tiled stove with a couple of easy chairs and a rocking chair in front of it. Next to the stove a small table. Engravings on the walls. An étagère with porcelain objects and other little art objects, a little book cupboard with books in showy bindings.[iii] A small daguerreotype of Nora's father and another of the Helmers' children. Carpet on the floor, a fire in the stove. A winter's day.[iv]

There is a ring out in the entry. The housemaid HELENE rushes in from the kitchen and exits to the entry. We hear the apartment door being unlocked.[v] NORA comes into the room humming, pleased and excited. She is dressed in outerwear[vi] and carries several packages, which she puts down on the table. Helene follows carrying a basket. The TOWN PORTER,[vii] who remains in the entry, carries a Christmas tree.[viii] Helene puts down the basket and takes the tree.

NORA: Hide the Christmas tree, Helene. I don't want the children to see it until tonight when it's lit.

> *(To the Porter as she takes out her coin purse)*

How much—?

TOWN PORTER: One *krone.*[ix]

NORA: Here's two.

> *He starts to give change, NORA stops him.*

Keep the change.[x]

PORTER: Oh, thank you!

> *PORTER exits. We hear the door shut behind him.[xi] NORA laughs softly, pleased, as she takes off her outerwear. She removes a bag of macaroons from her pocket and eats a couple. Cautiously, she goes over and listens by her husband's door.*

NORA: He's home.

> *She hums again and goes over to the table and begins to open the packages.*[xii]

HELMER *(off stage)*: Is that the song lark chirping out there? My little songbird?

NORA: Yes, it is.

HELMER *(off)*: Is that my squirrel[xiii] scurrying around?

NORA: Yes!

> *She puts the macaroon bag in her pocket and wipes her mouth.*

Come in here, Torvald, and see what I've bought.

HELMER *(off)*: I don't want to be disturbed!

> *Beat. HELMER opens the door and looks in, pen and papers in hand.*

Did you say bought? All that? Has my little bird been wasting money again?

NORA: Yes but, Torvald, this year we can spend a little more. It's the first Christmas we don't have to scrimp and save.

HELMER: But Nora, we can't just spend.

NORA: Oh, Torvald, of course we can. Can't we? Just a teeny tiny bit.

You're going to get a big salary and make lots and lots of money.

HELMER: Yes, after New Year's— but I won't be paid for three months.

NORA *(scoffs)*: We can borrow till then.

HELMER: Nora!

> *He goes over to her and puts his arm around her waist.*

Now then Little Miss Frivolous, suppose I borrowed a thousand *kroner* today and you spend every penny over Christmas. Then, on New Year's Eve, as I am walking down the street I get hit on the head by a falling roof tile and I lie there dyi—

> *She puts her hand over his mouth.*

NORA: Oh shush, if anything that awful happened, I'd be so devastated, I wouldn't care if I owed money or not.

HELMER: But what about the people I borrowed from?

NORA: Them? Who cares about them!— They're strangers.

HELMER: *Et tu*, Nora!

Seriously, you know what I think about that. No debt! Never borrow! A house built on debt can never be a beautiful home. Now, we've made it this long, we can brave it out a few more months.

> *She goes over to the stove.*

NORA: Yes, yes, as you wish, Torvald.

HELMER *(following after her)*: There, there. The little song lark mustn't droop her wings. What? Is my squirrel pouting?

He takes up his coin purse.

Nora, what do you think I have here?

NORA *(turns quickly)*: Money!

HELMER: That's right.

He hands her a few bills.

I know there's a lot of household expenses at Christmastime.

NORA: Ten— twenty— thirty— forty. Oh thank you, thank you, Torvald. I'll manage very well with this. But, come here and I'll show you what I've bought. And so cheaply too!

She opens the packages and admires the contents.

Here are new clothes for Ivar— and a sabre. A horse and a trumpet for Olaf. A doll and a doll bed for Emmy, it's so plain, but she'll quickly tear it apart anyway. And here, I have dress materials and shawls for the maids,[xiv] but Anne-Marie should really have something nicer.

HELMER: And what's in that package?

He moves to grab it.

She shrieks and grabs it back from him.

NORA: No, Torvald, you can't see *that* until this evening!

HELMER: I can't? But tell me, what do you have in mind for yourself?

NORA *(toying with his buttons, not looking up at him)*: If you wanted to give me something, then you could... you could—

HELMER: I could—?

NORA *(quickly)*: You could give me money, Torvald. Only as much as you think you can spare. And then, later on I'll buy something I need.

HELMER: Nora—

NORA: Oh yes, do it, dear Torvald, I *beg* you. I can hang the money in pretty, gold paper on the Christmas tree. Wouldn't that be fun?

HELMER *(smiling)*: Yes, if you could hang on to the money and really buy something for yourself with it. But, of course, you'll spend it on the house. And then I'll have to give you more.

NORA: Oh but, Torvald—

He puts his arm around her waist.

HELMER: You can't deny it, my dear little Nora— songbirds are sweet, but they spend a lot of money.

NORA *(hums and smiles, quietly pleased)*: Hm, if you only knew how many expenses we larks and squirrels have, Torvald.

HELMER: You're a strange little creature. Just like your father, very clever at getting money, but as soon as you have it— it slips through your fingers. Well, I must take you as you are. It's in your blood— it's inherited, Nora.

NORA: Aah,[xv] I wish I had inherited many of Papa's[xvi] other qualities.

HELMER: I wouldn't wish you *any* other way, my sweet little song lark. Wait a minute... you look so— so— so guilty today—

NORA: Do I?

HELMER: Oh yes, you do. Look me straight in the eyes.

NORA *(looks at him)*: Well?

HELMER *(threatens with his finger)*: Has Little Miss Sweet Tooth been loose in town today?

NORA: No, how can you think that?

HELMER: She didn't make a detour to the pastry shop?

NORA: No, Torvald—

HELMER: Not nibbled a macaroon or two?

NORA: No, Torvald, really I assure you—

HELMER: Of course I'm only joking—

NORA *(goes over to the table)*: I wouldn't dream of going against your wishes.

HELMER: I know. Besides, you promised—

> *He goes over to her.*

Well, you keep your little Christmas secrets to yourself, my darling. I'm sure they will be revealed tonight when the tree is lit.

NORA: You remembered to invite Dr. Rank?

HELMER: He'll be here. But I'll make sure and ask him when he comes by this morning. I've ordered a nice wine. Nora, you can't believe how much I am looking forward to tonight.

NORA: Me too. And the children will be so happy, Torvald!

HELMER: To think what I've achieved— a secure position, a generous income. I can't stop thinking about it. It's—

NORA: It's wonderful![xvii]

HELMER: Remember last Christmas? For three whole weeks you locked yourself in every night— to make flowers and decorations for the Christmas tree. Uh,[xviii] it was the most boring time I've ever lived through.

NORA: I wasn't bored at all.

HELMER *(smiling)*: And then the cat—

NORA: Oh, don't tease me! How could I know the cat would get in and tear everything to pieces?

HELMER: Of course you couldn't, my darling. You had the best intentions— to make us happy. I'm glad those lean times are over.

NORA: Yes, it's really wonderful. Now, I'll tell you what I've been thinking— as soon as Christmas is over—

A ring at the door.

Oh, there's the doorbell.

She straightens a little in the drawing room.

How annoying.[xix]

HELMER: Remember, I'm not home to visitors.

HELENE *(in the doorway to the entry)*: Ma'am, there's a strange lady here—

NORA: Yes, show her in.

HELENE *(to Helmer)*: And the Doctor came at the same time.

HELMER: Did he go straight in to my office?

HELENE: Yes, he did.

HELMER goes into his office. HELENE shows MRS. LINDE, who is dressed in a traveling clothes, into the room and closes the door after her.

MRS. LINDE *(hesitantly)*: Good day, Nora.

NORA *(uncertain)*: Good day—

MRS. LINDE: You probably don't recognize me.[xx]

NORA: No. I don't know— oh yes, I do think—

(Bursts out)

What! Kristine! Is it really you?[xxi]

MRS. LINDE: It's me.

NORA: Kristine! I didn't recognize you! But then how could I—

(Subdued)

You have changed, Kristine!

MRS. LINDE: I have. In nine... no, ten long years—

NORA: Has it been that long since we last saw each other? And now you've come to town? Made the long voyage in winter. That was brave.

MRS. LINDE: I came by steamer this morning.[xxii]

NORA: To enjoy the Christmas holiday, of course. Oh, that's lovely! But, take off your coat. You aren't cold, are you?

(Helping her)

Let's sit by the stove. No, in the armchair, it's more comfortable!

She sits in the rocker and grasps MRS. LINDE's hands.

NORA (CONT'D): Now you look like your old self, it was just that first moment— But you've gotten a little paler, Kristine— and perhaps a little thinner.

MRS. LINDE: And much, much older, Nora.

NORA: Perhaps a little older— a teeny tiny bit— not much at all.

> *(Suddenly stops, seriously)*

Oh, how thoughtless of me. I'm sitting here talking! Dear, sweet Kristine, can you forgive me?

MRS. LINDE: What do you mean?

NORA *(softly)*: Poor Kristine, you've become a widow.

MRS. LINDE: Yes, three years ago.

NORA: Oh, of course I knew, I read about it in the papers. Oh you must believe me, I often thought of writing to you, but I always postponed it. Something always got in the way.

MRS. LINDE: Dear Nora, I understand completely.

NORA: No, it was bad of me. Oh, you poor thing, you've gone through so much— And he didn't leave you anything to live on?

MRS. LINDE: No.

NORA *(looking at the gifts for her children)*: And no children?

MRS. LINDE: No.

NORA: Nothing at all?

MRS. LINDE: Nothing. Not even grief to occupy my thoughts.

NORA *(looks at her doubtfully)*: Kristine, how is that possible?

MRS. LINDE *(smiles heavily, stroking Nora's hair)*: Oh, it happens now and then.

NORA: So absolutely alone. How terrible that must be for you. I have three beautiful children. Well, you can't see them right now because they are out with their nanny, old Anne-Marie. But now you must tell me all—

MRS. LINDE: No, no, no, you tell me—

NORA: No, you must begin. Today I don't want to be selfish. Today I only want to think of you. I must tell you one thing though. Do you know about our great good fortune?

MRS. LINDE: No. What is it?

NORA: My husband has been made the Director of the Stock Bank![xxiii]

MRS. LINDE: Your husband? How lucky—!

NORA: Yes, enormously lucky! It was so hard for Torvald to make a living as a lawyer. He never liked being associated with anything shady or unsavory— and I completely agree with him.

NORA (CONT'D): So, you can imagine how happy we are with this new position at the bank! He starts on New Year's, and then he will get a big salary and a... a bo...

MRS. LINDE: A bonus?

NORA: Yes, a bonus! Well, after that we can live just as we want. Oh, Kristine, I'm so happy! It's lovely, isn't it, to have lots of money and not have to worry.

MRS. LINDE: Yes it must be lovely to have enough to live on.

NORA: Not only enough, but lots and lots of money!

MRS. LINDE *(smiles)*: Nora, Nora, haven't you grown up? At school you were always so careless with money.

NORA *(laughs quietly)*: Yes, that's what Torvald still says.

> She threatens with her finger.

But "Nora, Nora" isn't as silly as you all think. —Oh, we've had to be very careful. We've had to work, both of us.

MRS. LINDE: You too?

NORA: Yes, with little things— handcraft, crocheting, embroidery[xxiv] and such,

> (Hinting)

and with other things, too. You know Torvald left the government after we were married? He needed a better salary and there was no hope of advancement in that office. That first year, he worked so terribly hard and took on all kinds of extra work. He worked from early morning to late at night. But, his constitution couldn't take it, and he got terribly sick. The doctors said it was necessary for him to go to the south of Europe.

MRS. LINDE: You stayed a whole year in Italy, didn't you?

NORA: Yes. It wasn't easy to get away. Ivar had just been born. But, we had to go. Oh, it was a wonderful journey. It saved Torvald's life. But, it cost a lot of money, Kristine.

MRS. LINDE: I can well imagine.

NORA: Four thousand eight hundred *kroner*. That's a lot of money.

MRS. LINDE: How lucky you had it.

NORA: We got it from my father.

MRS. LINDE: But, didn't your father die around that time?

NORA: Yes he did. It was so hard, Kristine. I couldn't go to Papa and nurse him. I was here waiting every day for Ivar to be born. And I had my poor sick Torvald to take care of. My dear kind Papa! I never saw him again, Kristine.

MRS. LINDE: I know you were very fond of him. But, then you traveled to Italy?

NORA: Yes, we left just a month later.

MRS. LINDE: And your husband came back completely cured?

NORA: Healthy as a horse!

MRS. LINDE: But— the doctor?

NORA: What?

MRS. LINDE: I think the maid said he was a doctor— the gentleman who arrived at the same time as I did.

NORA: That's Dr. Rank— but he doesn't come here on house calls, he's our closest friend, and he comes by at least once a day. No, Torvald hasn't had a sick hour since. And the children are healthy, and me too.

She jumps up and claps her hands.

Oh God, oh God, Kristine, it's really wonderful to be alive and happy, isn't it! —Oh, how awful of me— I'm only talking about myself.

Sits down on a footstool close to MRS. LINDE and puts her arms on Mrs. Linde's knee.

Oh, don't be angry with me! —You really didn't love your husband? Why did you marry him then?

MRS. LINDE: My mother was still alive, but she was bedridden and helpless. I also had my two younger brothers to support. I didn't think I could reject his offer.

NORA: No, no, you may be right about that. So, he was rich?

MRS. LINDE: He was fairly well off. But the business world is very uncertain, Nora. When he died, the whole thing went under and there was nothing left.

NORA: And then—?

MRS. LINDE: Well, then I had to manage with whatever I could find, a small shop and then a small school. [xxv] The last three years have felt like one long workday without any rest. Now it's over, Nora. My poor mother doesn't need me anymore— she passed away. And the boys don't either. They have found work and can support themselves.

NORA: You must feel so relie—

MRS. LINDE: No, only unspeakably empty. Nobody to live for any more.

Stands up, uneasy.

That's why I couldn't endure it up there any longer in that little backwater. It must be easier to find something down here that can fill my days and occupy my thoughts. If only I could be lucky enough to get a permanent position, some office work—

NORA: Oh, but Kristine, that is so terribly hard, and you look so worn out. It would be much better for you if you could go to a spa.

MRS. LINDE walks over to the window.

MRS. LINDE: I have no "papa" to give me the travel money, Nora.

NORA gets up.

NORA: Oh, don't be angry with me!

MRS. LINDE *(over to Nora)*: Dear Nora, don't you be angry with me. The worst thing with a situation like mine— it fills you with so much bitterness. No one to work for— but still pinching pennies— and then you become... selfish. When you told me about your good fortune— would you believe it— I was glad not so much for you as for me.

NORA: How so? Oh, you mean that Torvald might be able to do something for you.

MRS. LINDE: Yes, that's what I was thinking.

NORA: And he will, Kristine. Just leave it all to me. I will introduce it so subtly, so subtly— think of something to tempt him... Oh, I really want to help you.

MRS. LINDE: That's so kind of you, Nora— especially since *you* know so little of life's burdens.

NORA: I—? I know so little of—?

MRS. LINDE *(smiling)*: Well, good Lord, a little handcraft and such?— You're a child, Nora.

> *NORA tosses her head and walks across the floor.*

NORA: Don't be so condescending.

MRS. LINDE: Nora—

NORA: You're like the others. You all think that I'm not capable of doing anything really serious—

MRS. LINDE: But Nora you just told me all your troubles.

NORA: *Ha*— those trifles!

> *(Softly)*

I haven't told you about the big thing.

MRS. LINDE: What big thing?

NORA: You look down on me, Kristine. You shouldn't do that—

MRS. LINDE: I don't look down on anyone—

NORA: You're proud of having worked so long and hard for your mother and brothers.

MRS. LINDE: Yes.

NORA: I have something to be proud of too.

MRS. LINDE: Yes? But, what is it?

NORA: Hush! Think, if Torvald heard! No one can know, Kristine— no one but you.

> *NORA pulls her down onto the sofa next to herself.*

It was me. I saved Torvald's life.

MRS. LINDE: Saved—? Saved how?

NORA: I told you about the trip to Italy. Torvald would not have survived if we hadn't—

MRS. LINDE: But, your father gave you the money—

NORA *(smiles)*: Yes, that's what Torvald and all the others think, but— Papa gave us nothing.[xxvi] It was me. I came up with the money.

MRS. LINDE: You? The whole amount?

NORA: Four-thousand eight-hundred *kroner*. What do you think of that?

MRS. LINDE: But where did you get it?

NORA *(hums and smiles secretively)*: Hm— tra la la la!

MRS. LINDE: Because you couldn't borrow it.

NORA: Oh? Why not?

MRS. LINDE: A wife cannot borrow without her husband's consent.[xxvii]

NORA: Who says I *borrowed* the money. I might've gotten it some other way.

She throws herself on the sofa.

I might've gotten it from an admirer. When you're as attractive as I am—

MRS. LINDE: Have you lost your mind?

NORA: I think you are dying of curiosity, Kristine.

MRS. LINDE: Nora— you haven't done anything foolish?

NORA *(sitting upright again)*: Was it foolish to save my husband's life?

MRS. LINDE: It seems to me that it was foolish, without his knowledge, to—

NORA: For God's sake, he couldn't even be told how seriously ill he was. The doctors came to *me* and said that his life was in danger— that nothing could save him but a trip south. Do you think I didn't try to cajole him at first? I talked to him about how lovely it would be to go abroad like other young wives— I cried, I pleaded— I reminded him about my condition and that he should humor me. Finally, I suggested that we take out a loan. He got angry, Kristine. He said that I was irresponsible and that it was his duty as my husband not to humor me in my "whims and caprices"— that's what he called them. I thought to myself, yes, you must be saved— and I came up with a way to—

MRS. LINDE: And you never told your husband?

NORA: No, for Heaven's sake. Torvald and his male ego— it would be painful and humiliating for him to know that he owed me anything. It would wreck our relationship— destroy our beautiful happy home.

MRS. LINDE: Will you ever tell him?

NORA *(thoughtful, half smiling)*: Yes— one day— maybe— many years from now, when I am no longer as pretty as I am now. Don't laugh! Then it might be good to have something up my sleeve—

She brushes away the thought.

NORA (CONT'D): Well, what do you say about my secret, Kristine? Am I not useful, too?— It's not been easy to make my payments on time. In the business world there is something called quarter interest, and something called installments— and they are always very hard to make. I've had to save a little here and there, when I could. I couldn't use much of the household money, because Torvald had to live well. I couldn't let the children go badly dressed. The sweet darlings!

So every time Torvald gave me money for new dresses and things for myself, I never used more than half— always bought the simplest and cheapest. It's a godsend that everything looks good on me— Torvald didn't notice. It's been a burden, Kristine— because it is, after all, lovely to walk around beautifully dressed.

MRS. LINDE: Oh yes it is.

NORA: I had *other* sources of income too. Last winter, I was lucky to get a lot of copy work. I locked myself away and sat there and wrote every evening until late at night. Many times I was so tired, so tired. But, it was still tremendous[xxviii] fun to sit like that and work and earn money. It was almost as if I were a man.

MRS. LINDE: How much have you been able to pay off?

NORA: *Weeell*, I can't tell exactly. It's very hard to keep track. I only know that I have paid everything that I could scrape together. Many times I couldn't figure out how I would make the next payment.

> *(Smiles)*

Sometimes I would sit here and imagine that a rich old gentleman had fallen in love with me—

MRS. LINDE: What gentleman?

NORA: —and he would die and when they opened his will, it would say there in big letters "All my money shall be paid out immediately in cash to the loveable Mrs. Nora Helmer."

MRS. LINDE: But dear Nora— what gentleman?

NORA: Good Heavens— he doesn't exist!— it was only something I imagined over and over again, when I couldn't figure out how to get money. But, now I have no worries.

> *She jumps up.*

Can you imagine, Kristine?! To be worry free— Oh yes, yes, it's wonderful to be alive and happy!

> *The doorbell rings in the entry.*

MRS. LINDE *(gets up):* Maybe I had better go.

NORA: No, you stay, I get very few visitors—[xxix] I suppose it's for Torvald—

HELENE *(in the door to the entry)*: Excuse me, Mrs.,ˣˣ— there's a gentleman here who wants to talk with the attorney—

NORA: With the Bank Director, you mean.

HELENE: Yes, with the Bank Director. But, I didn't know— the Doctor is in there—

NORA: Who is the gentleman?

KROGSTAD *(in the doorway to the entry)*: It's me, Mrs. Helmer.

> *MRS. LINDE starts, shrinks, and turns toward the window.*

NORA *(takes a step toward him, tensely, with a half voice)*: You? What is it? What do You want to talk to my husband about?

KROGSTAD: Bank business— in a way. I hear that Torvald— that Your husband is going to be our new director—

NORA: So it is...

KROGSTAD: —Only routine business, Mrs. Helmer, nothing more.

NORA: Yes, would You be so kind as to go in through the office door.

> *NORA takes brief leave of him in a deliberately casual, unengaged way, closing the door to the entry after him. She goes over and tends the stove.*

MRS. LINDE: Nora— who was that man?

NORA: That was this... just a lawyer, Krogstad.

MRS. LINDE: So, it really was him.

NORA: Do you know that person?

MRS. LINDE: Yes, I used to know him— some years ago. He was a law clerk up there where I lived.

NORA: Oh, yes, that's right.

MRS. LINDE: He's changed.

NORA: I think he had a very unhappy marriage.

MRS. LINDE: He's a widower now, right?

NORA: With many children. There, now. Now it's catching.

> *NORA closes the door of the stove and moves the rocking chair a little to the side.*

MRS. LINDE: They say he was involved with all kinds of different businesses?

NORA: Yes, I suppose, I really don't know— But let's not talk of business, it's so boring.

> *DR RANK enters from Helmer's office.*

DR. RANK *(still in the doorway)*: No no, I don't want to be in the way. I'd rather see your wife.

DR. RANK (CONT'D) *(notices Mrs. Linde)*: Oh, excuse me. I guess I'm in the way here too.

NORA: No, not at all

    (Introducing)

Dr. Rank. Mrs. Linde.

RANK: Linde. A name that is often heard in this house. I think I passed the lady on[xxxi] the stairs when I came up.

MRS. LINDE: Yes. I climb stairs very slowly.

RANK: Ah, having a little internal trouble?[xxxii]

MRS. LINDE: Just overworked.

RANK: Is that all? So, You've come to town to rest up at all the Christmas parties?

MRS. LINDE: I've come to seek employment.

RANK: Is that the right cure for overwork?

MRS. LINDE: We all must live, Doctor.

RANK: Yes, it's a generally held opinion.

NORA: Oh, shame on You, Dr. Rank— really, You want to live as much as the next person.

RANK: Yes, I do. However pitiful I am, I would like to continue being plagued for as long as possible. All my patients feel the same way. Even the morally rotten ones want to live. Right now, there's one such case in there with Helmer—

MRS. LINDE *(subdued)*: Ah!

NORA: Who do You mean?

RANK: Oh, it's this lawyer, Krogstad, someone You don't know at all. He is rotted to the core, Mrs. Helmer. But, even he just now was making the grand statement, "We all must live."

NORA: So, what did he want to talk to Torvald about?

RANK: I honestly don't know. It was something about the Stock Bank.

NORA: I didn't know that Krog— that this lawyer, Krogstad, had anything to do with the Bank.

RANK: Yes, he's got some kind of employment there.

       NORA, in her own thoughts, bursts out in half-loud laughter and claps her hands.

NORA: Tell me, Dr. Rank— from now on everyone employed in the bank will answer to Torvald?

RANK: You find that funny?

NORA *(smiles and hums)*: Yes, it's enormously[xxxiii] amusing. To think that we— that Torvald— has so much influence on so many people.

NORA (CONT'D) *(to Mrs. Linde)*: Leave it to me.

> *She takes the bag out of her pocket.*

Dr. Rank, would You like a macaroon.

RANK: A-ha, macaroons. I thought they were contraband here.

NORA: Yes, but Kristine gave me these.

MRS. LINDE: What? I—?

NORA: Well, well, well, don't be alarmed. You couldn't know that Torvald has forbidden them. He's afraid they'll rot my teeth. But for once—! Isn't that true, Dr. Rank? Be so good!

> *She puts a macaroon in his mouth.*

And you too, Kristine. And I will also have one, only a little one— or at the most two.

> *(Parading)*

Yes, I am incredibly happy. Right now there is just one thing I have an enormous desire to do.

RANK: Well? What is that?

NORA: I have an enormous desire to say something and have Torvald hear me say it.

RANK: So why can't You say it?

NORA: No, I don't dare, it's so ugly.

MRS. LINDE: Ugly?

RANK: Well, then it's not advisable. But, surely You can tell us...

NORA: I have an enormous desire to say: "Goddammit to hell."[xxxiv]

RANK: Are You insane!

MRS. LINDE: Goodness sakes, Nora—!

RANK: Here he comes. Say it.

NORA *(hides the macaroon bag)*: Sh, sh, sh!

> *HELMER, with overcoat on his arm and hat in hand, comes from his office.*

Well, Torvald dear, did you get rid of him?

HELMER: Yes, he left.

NORA: Torvald, may I introduce[xxxv]— this is Kristine who has just arrived in town— Mrs. Kristine Linde.

HELMER: Ah so. Presumably a childhood friend of my wife's?

MRS. LINDE: Yes, we knew each other when we were girls.

NORA: She's made the long journey into town for a chance to talk to you.

HELMER: About what?

MRS. LINDE: Yes, I... really—

NORA: Kristine, you see, is enormously clever at office work, and she has a tremendous desire to be under the guidance of a capable man and learn more—

HELMER: Very sensible, Mrs. Linde.

NORA: When she heard that you had become a bank director— there was a telegram about that[xxxvi]— she traveled as quickly as she could to town and— You can do some little thing for Kristine, for my sake, can't you?

HELMER: It's not at all impossible. I presume Mrs. Linde is a widow?

MRS. LINDE: Yes.

HELMER: And has experience with office work?

MRS. LINDE: Yes, quite a bit.

HELMER: In that case, it's very likely that I can get You employment—

NORA (claps her hands): There you see!

HELMER: You have come at a fortunate moment, Mrs. Linde—

MRS. LINDE: Oh, how can I thank You—?

HELMER: No need.

> He pulls on his overcoat.

But, today You must excuse me—

RANK: Wait, I'll go with you.

> Collects his fur coat[xxxvii] from the entry and warms it by the stove.

NORA: Don't stay out too long.

HELMER: One hour, no more.

NORA: Are you leaving, too, Kristine?

MRS. LINDE (putting on her outerwear): Yes, I must go look for a room.

HELMER: We will walk down the street together.[xxxviii]

MRS. LINDE: Goodbye, dear Nora, and thank you for everything.

NORA: Goodbye for now! You will, of course, come back this evening. And You too, Dr. Rank.

> RANK voices an unheard objection.

Just stay warm!

> ANNE-MARIE enters with Emmy's coat and the children's knitted scarves and sweaters and brings them to the nursery. Children's voices are heard on the stairs and from the entry.

NORA (calling off stage): Here they come!

HELMER *(exiting)*: Come, Mrs. Linde— this place is no longer endurable to anyone other than mothers.

> *DR. RANK, HELMER, and MRS. LINDE leave.*

NORA: Kristine— Look at them, Kristine. Aren't they lovely! My sweet, healthy, brave darlings—

> *She sees the Christmas gifts.*

Oh no, no— you can't come in here. Go warm yourselves in the kitchen, you look so frozen.

> *(To Anne-Marie)*

There is coffee on the kitchen stove for you.

> *(To the children)*

When you get your indoor shoes on we'll play hide and seek.

ANNE-MARIE *(exiting)*: Come on my dears, to the kitchen. Oh no you don't. You can't go through that way. Your Mamma said no.

NORA: Go around to the kitchen!

> *NORA laughs and covers up the Christmas gifts for the children with the tablecloth, making sure they can't see them. She moves a small table and chair to make room for the Christmas tree.*
>
> *She calls off stage. During the counting, KROGSTAD enters.*

NORA *(calls)*: Are you ready?

ANNE-MARIE: They're ready!

NORA: Go hide! Go hide!

> *She covers her eyes.*

One-2-3-4-5-6-7-8-9-10. Ready or not, here I—

KROGSTAD: Excuse me, Mrs. Helmer—

> *NORA suppresses a scream, turns, half jumps up.*

NORA: Ah! What do *You* want?

KROGSTAD: Sorry, the door was— somebody must have left it open—

NORA *(gets up)*: My husband is not home, Mr. Krogstad.

KROGSTAD: I know.

NORA: Yes then— what do *You* want?

KROGSTAD: To speak with *You*.

NORA: With—?

> *(Calls off stage)*

Anne-Marie!

ANNE-MARIE appears in the doorway, holding a pair of wet socks.

NORA: Tell the children I have a visitor. I will play with them as soon as he's gone.

ANNE-MARIE: Yes, Mrs. Nora.

(Exiting)

Oh, Olaf!

NORA sees Olaf in the doorway and dashes over to him.

NORA: Olaf, my sweetheart, go with Anne-Marie to the kitchen. What? No, the strange man isn't going to hurt Mamma. When he has gone, I promise we'll play.

NORA returns to the room.

(Anxious)

You want to speak with me?

KROGSTAD: Yes.

NORA: Today—? But it's not the first of the month yet—

KROGSTAD: I know. It's Christmas Eve.

NORA: What do You want?

KROGSTAD: I was sitting in Olsen's restaurant and saw Your husband walking down the street—

NORA: Yes.

KROGSTAD: —with a lady.

NORA: So?

KROGSTAD: May I be so bold as to ask— Was that lady a Mrs. Linde?

NORA: Yes.

KROGSTAD: Just come to town?

NORA: Yes, today.

KROGSTAD: She is a good friend of Yours, isn't she?

NORA: Yes, she is. But I don't understand—

KROGSTAD: I also knew her once.

NORA: I know.

KROGSTAD: So? You know about that. I thought as much. May I ask You, will Mrs. Linde be employed at the Stock Bank?

NORA: Yes, Mrs. Linde will have a position there. I'm the one who spoke on her behalf, Mr. Krogstad. Now You know.

KROGSTAD: So I added it all up correctly.

NORA *(pacing)*: I do have a little bit of influence. A subordinate like You, Mr. Krogstad, really needs to be careful not to offend anyone, who—

KROGSTAD: —who has influence?

NORA: Precisely.

KROGSTAD *(changes tone)*: Mrs. Helmer, would You be good enough to use Your influence on my behalf.

NORA: What? What do You mean?

KROGSTAD: Would You be so kind as to make sure I keep my subordinate position at the bank.

NORA: Who is taking Your position from You?

KROGSTAD: Oh, You don't have to pretend. I see that Your friend doesn't want to risk running into me. I also see who I have to thank for being dismissed.

NORA: But, I assure You—

KROGSTAD: Yes, yes, yes, here's my point— there is still time and I advise You to use Your influence to prevent it.

NORA: But, Mr. Krogstad, I *have* no influence.

KROGSTAD: You don't? You just said—

NORA: Of course, I didn't mean it like that! How can You think that I would have that kind of influence over my husband?

KROGSTAD: Oh, I know Your husband. We were at law school together. I don't think Mr. Bank Director is any more principled than other married men.

NORA: If you speak with contempt about my husband I will show You the door.

KROGSTAD: The lady has spirit.

NORA: I am no longer afraid of You. After the New Year, I will be out from under all this.

KROGSTAD *(in control)*: Now listen to me, Mrs. Helmer. If it becomes necessary, to keep my position at the bank I will fight to the death.

NORA: Yes, so it would seem.

KROGSTAD: It's not for the sake of the money— that's the least important thing to me. It's something else— You know that once, a number of years ago, I was guilty of an indiscretion.

NORA: I think I heard something about that.

KROGSTAD: The thing did not go to trial— but all doors were immediately closed to me. I had no choice but to go into all these various— side businesses. I had to do something— and I have to say, I was not among the worst. But now, I want out of it. My sons are growing up. For their sake, I must regain as much middle class respectability as I can. This modest position in the bank was the first step on the ladder for me. And now Your husband wants to kick it out from under me, plunging me back into the gutter.

NORA: For God's sake, Mr. Krogstad, it is absolutely not in my power to help You.

KROGSTAD: Because You don't want to— but I can force You to.

NORA: You won't tell my husband that I owe You money?

KROGSTAD: What if I do?[xxxix]

NORA: That would be a shameful thing to do.

(With tears caught in her throat)

This secret is my joy and my pride. If he found out in such an ugly and coarse way— be told about it by *You*. It would be terribly unpleasant.

KROGSTAD: Unpleasant?

NORA: If my husband finds out, he'll immediately pay off the rest of my loan.

KROGSTAD *(one step closer)*: Listen, Mrs. Helmer— either you have a bad memory, or you have no real understanding of business. Let me explain things more thoroughly.

When Your husband was sick, You came to me to borrow 4,800 *kroner*.

NORA: I didn't know where else to turn.

KROGSTAD: I promised to get You the money against a promissory note, which I drafted.

NORA: Yes, and I signed.

KROGSTAD: Good. But, at the bottom I added a few lines and a clause stating that Your father would guarantee the debt. Your father was going to sign on those lines.

NORA: Was going to—? But he did sign.

KROGSTAD: I left the date blank— Your father would date his own signature. Do You remember that, Mrs. Helmer?

NORA: Yes, I think so—

KROGSTAD: Then I gave the promissory note to You so that You could mail it to Your father. Wasn't that so?

NORA: Yes.

KROGSTAD: You did that right away because about five or six days later You brought me the note with Your father's signature. And then You received the money.

NORA: Haven't I made payments regularly?

KROGSTAD: Reasonably well, yes. But— to return to the topic at hand— this was a difficult time for You, Mrs. Helmer?

NORA: Yes it was.

KROGSTAD: Your father was very ill, I think.

NORA: He was on his deathbed. He was dying.

KROGSTAD: Died not too long after that, right?

NORA: Yes.

KROGSTAD: Mrs. Helmer, do you perhaps remember the day of Your father's death? What day of the month it was, I mean.

NORA: Papa died September 29th.

KROGSTAD: That's right. I made inquiries about that. So, there is a peculiarity

He takes out a paper.

that I just can't explain.

NORA: What peculiarity? I don't know—

KROGSTAD: Here is the peculiarity, Mrs. Helmer, Your father signed the promissory note three days after his death.

NORA: How? I don't understand—

KROGSTAD: Your father died on September 29th. But look here. Here Your father dated his signature October 2nd. Isn't that peculiar, Mrs. Helmer?

NORA is silent.

Can You explain that?

NORA is still silent.

It is important to note that the words "October 2nd" and the year are not written in Your father's hand. Well, that can be easily explained, Your father could've forgotten to date his signature and then someone else randomly wrote a date here before they knew he had died. There is nothing wrong with that. It is the signature this hinges on. That is genuine, isn't it, Mrs. Helmer? It really was Your father who signed his name?

NORA (*after a brief silence, tossing her head, and looking at him defiantly*): No, it wasn't. It was *me.* I wrote Papa's name.

KROGSTAD: Mrs. Helmer, You realize that this is a dangerous admission?

NORA: Why? You will soon have Your money.

KROGSTAD: May I ask You a question?— Why didn't You send the note to Your father?

NORA: It was impossible. Papa was in bed sick. If I had asked for his signature, I'd have to tell him what the money was for.

KROGSTAD: Then You should have given up that trip abroad.

NORA: That trip was to save my husband's life.

KROGSTAD: Didn't it occur to You that You were defrauding *me*—?

NORA: I couldn't concern myself with that. I didn't care about You at all— all the difficulties You put me through even though You knew how dangerously ill my husband was.

KROGSTAD: Mrs. Helmer, You obviously have no idea what it is You're guilty of. But let me tell you, what you have done is neither better nor worse than what I did, just once, and it ruined my entire position in society.

NORA: You? You want me to believe that You did something brave to save Your wife's life?

KROGSTAD: The laws don't ask about motivations.

NORA: Then they must be very bad laws.

KROGSTAD: Bad or not— if I show this paper in court, You will be judged according to them.

NORA: I don't think so. Shouldn't a daughter have the right to spare her dying father anxiety and worry? Shouldn't a wife have the right to save her husband's life? I don't know the laws so well, but I am sure such things are allowed. And You're a lawyer? You must be a bad one, Mr. Krogstad.

KROGSTAD: That may be. But the business we're in together— You know I'm good at that. Now do whatever You want. But let me tell You this— if I am cast out of society for the second time, You will keep me company.

He takes his leave and goes out through the entry.

NORA *(for a while thoughtful; then tosses her head)*: Trying to scare me.

She begins to fold the children's clothes; soon stops.

But—? —No, but sure it is impossible! I did it for love.

ANNE-MARIE enters.

ANNE-MARIE: Mrs. Nora, Ivar says he saw the strange man leave.

NORA: Tell Ivar not to talk about the strange man to anyone. Not to his Pappa either. Do you hear?

ANNE-MARIE: Yes, Mrs. Nora— The children want to know if you'll play with them now.

NORA: No, no— not now.

ANNE MARIE: Oh but, Mrs. Nora— you did promise.

NORA: I can't now. I have so much to do. You stay with them, dear Anne-Marie.

ANNE-MARIE goes. NORA sits down in the sofa, takes up a piece of needlework and takes a few stitches, soon stops.

NORA: No!

Tosses the embroidery aside, gets up, goes to the door to the entry and calls out.

Helene! Bring the tree in here.

Goes to the small table and opens the table drawer; stops again.

No, it is absolutely impossible!

HELENE *(with the tree and a small basket of Christmas decorations)*: Where should I put it, Ma'am?

NORA *(she points)*: There.

> *HELENE puts the tree and basket down.*

HELENE: Should I get anything else?

NORA: No, thank you. I have what I need.

> *HELENE goes out. NORA begins to decorate the tree.*

Candles here— flowers here— That horrible person— There is nothing wrong. The Christmas tree will be beautiful.

> *HELMER, with a packet of papers under his arm, comes in from the entry.*

NORA: Oh— are you back already?

HELMER: Yes. Has someone been here?

NORA: Here? No.

HELMER: That's strange. I just saw Krogstad leave the building.

NORA: Really? Oh yes, of course, Krogstad was here, for a moment.

HELMER: Nora, I can tell by looking at you. He was here, begging you to put in a good word for him.

NORA: Yes.

HELMER: And you were going to act like it was your own idea? You were going to keep his visit a secret from me. Did he beg for that too?

NORA: Yes, Torvald, but—

HELMER: Nora, Nora, and you let yourself go along with that? Talk with someone like him, and make him a promise! And to top it off, lie to me!

NORA: Lie—?

HELMER: Didn't you say that no one had been here?

> *He shakes his finger at her.*

My little songbird must never do *that* again. A songbird must sing pure and clear— never false notes.

> *He puts his arm around her waist.*

Isn't that the way it should be? Yes, I know it is.

> *He lets go of her and sits down in front of the stove.*

Oh, how warm and cozy it is in here.

> *He leafs through his papers a little.*

NORA *(busy with the Christmas tree; after a brief pause)*: Torvald!

HELMER: Yes.

NORA: I am enormously excited about the costume party at the Stenborg's the day after tomorrow.

HELMER: And I am *enormously* eager to see what you are going to surprise me with.

NORA *(behind his chair, with her arms on the back of the chair)*: Are you very busy, Torvald?

HELMER: I persuaded the board of directors to give me full authority to make all the necessary changes in staff and administrative procedures. I want to have everything in order by New Year's.

NORA: So that's why poor Krogstad—

HELMER: Hm.

NORA *(still leaning on the back of the chair, slowly strokes the hair on his neck)*: If you weren't so busy, I would ask you for an enormously big favor, Torvald.

HELMER: What might that be?

NORA: No one has your good taste. I'd like to look good at the costume party. Torvald, will you take me under your wing and help decide what costume I should wear?

HELMER: I'll think about it. We'll come up with something.

NORA: Thank you, dear.

Goes over to the Christmas tree again; pause.

How pretty the red flowers look— But tell me, what is this Krogstad guilty of, is it really so bad?

HELMER: Forgery. Do you have any idea what that means?

NORA: Couldn't he have done it out of sheer need?

HELMER: Or out of thoughtlessness, like so many others. I am not so heartless as to unconditionally condemn a man because of a single act.

NORA: No, I know you're not!

HELMER: A man can get on his feet again by openly confessing his crime and enduring his punishment.

NORA: Punishment—?

HELMER: But, Krogstad didn't take that path. He manipulated the situation to his advantage with tricks and schemes— and it's corrupted him, morally.

NORA: Do you think that it would—?

HELMER: Just imagine how a person like him must lie and pretend to everyone around him— must wear a mask for his nearest and dearest— yes even for his own wife and children. And this thing with the *children*— that's the *most* dreadful part, Nora.

NORA: Why?

HELMER: Because such a miasma of lies brings contagion and sickness into a home. Every breath his children take is filled with the germs of something... ugly.

NORA *(closer behind him)*: Are you sure of that?

HELMER: My dear, I saw enough of that when I was a lawyer. Almost everyone corrupted early in life had a deceitful mother.

NORA: Why only— the mother?

HELMER: It derives mostly from the mother— but fathers, of course, have the same influence, every lawyer knows that. For years, this Krogstad has been poisoning his own children with lies and deception— that's why he's morally corrupt.

>   *He reaches out his hands toward her.*

So, my sweet little Nora, promise me not to plead his case. Your hand on that.

Well, well what is this? Give me your hand. There now. That's settled then.

I assure you it would be impossible to work with him. I become physically ill in the presence of someone like that.

>   *NORA pulls back her hand and goes over to the other side of the Christmas tree.*

NORA: It's hot in here. And I have so much to take care of.

HELMER *(gets up and pulls his papers together)*: And I must read this before dinner and think about your costume. And, maybe, I'll have something to hang in gold paper on the Christmas tree.

>   *He lays his hand on her head.*

Oh, you, my sweet little songbird.

>   *HELMER goes into his office and closes the door.*

ANNE-MARIE *(entering)*: The little ones are asking so sweetly if they can come in to their Mamma now.

NORA: No, no, no— don't let them come in here! You stay with them, Anne-Marie.

ANNE-MARIE: Yes, yes, Mrs. Nora.

>   *She leaves.*

NORA *(pale with fright)*: Corrupt my little children—! Poison the home?

>   *Brief pause; she lifts her head.*

This is not true. This can never be true. Never. Ever.

ACT I, SCENE 2

Christmas Day. The same room. In the corner next to the piano stands the Christmas tree,[xl] picked over, disheveled, and with burnt down candles.[xli] Ivar's sabre and Emmy's mutilated doll lie on the floor near the tree. Nora's outerwear lies on the sofa.

NORA, alone in the room, walks around uneasily. Finally she stops by the sofa and picks up her cloak. She hears a sound and looks toward the entry.

NORA *(listens for a moment)*: Nobody. Of course— nobody will come today, it's Christmas Day[xlii]; maybe—

She opens the door and looks at the mailbox in the entry.

nothing in the mailbox—

She walks back into the room.

Oh, nonsense!

ANNE-MARIE, with a large cardboard box, comes in.

ANNE-MARIE: Well, I finally found the box[xliii] with the masquerade costumes.

NORA: Thank you. Put it on the table.

ANNE-MARIE *(does so)*: They're very jumbled.

NORA: Oh, I want to tear it all into a hundred thousand pieces!

ANNE-MARIE: Goodness gracious— they can easily be put in order. Just a little patience.

NORA: I'll go and get Mrs. Linde to help me.

ANNE-MARIE *(begins straightening up the room)*: Out again? In this nasty weather? Mrs. Nora[xliv] will catch a cold— get sick.

NORA: Oh, worse things could happen— How are the children doing?

ANNE-MARIE: The poor little bugs are playing with their Christmas presents, but—

NORA: Are they asking for me?

ANNE-MARIE: They're so used to having their Mamma around.

NORA: From now on I *can't* be with them as much.

ANNE-MARIE: Well, little children get used to anything.

NORA: Do you think so? Do you think they'd forget their mother if she was gone?

ANNE-MARIE: Goodness gracious— gone!

NORA: Tell me Anne-Marie— I've often wondered, how could you leave your child with strangers?

ANNE-MARIE: But I had to, didn't I, when I became little Nora's wet-nurse.

NORA: But didn't it break your heart?

ANNE-MARIE: When I could get such a good position? A poor girl who has gotten herself into trouble can't pass up such an offer. Besides, that good-for-nothing wouldn't do a thing for me.

NORA: But, hasn't your daughter forgotten you?

ANNE-MARIE: Oh no! She wrote to me, both when she was confirmed and when she got married.

> *NORA throws her arms around ANNE-MARIE's neck.*

NORA: Dear old Anne-Marie, you were a good mother to me.

ANNE-MARIE: Little Nora, poor thing, didn't have any other mother but me.[xlv]

NORA: And if my little ones didn't have any other, then I know that you would— Talk, talk, talk.

> *She opens the box.*

Go in to them. Now I must— Tomorrow you'll see how pretty I'll look.

ANNE-MARIE: Yes, there will be nobody at the whole ball[xlvi] as pretty as Mrs. Nora.

> *ANNE-MARIE exits to the nursery.*

> *NORA begins to unpack the box, but soon throws it all down.*

NORA: No one is coming. Silly talk—

> *(Plays with her muff and gloves)*

Push it away; push it away! One, two, three, four, five, six—

> *She screams.*

Oh, they're coming—

> *Wants to go to the door but remains standing indecisive.*

> *MRS. LINDE comes in from the entry, where she has taken off her outerwear.*

NORA: Oh, Kristine it's you. There's no one else out there?— Thank goodness you're here.

MRS. LINDE: I heard you came by asking for me.

NORA: Yes, I was just passing by.

There is something you absolutely have to help me with. Let's sit down.

> *NORA sees the doll under the tree and retrieves it. She and MRS. LINDE share a look.*

NORA (CONT'D): There's going to be a costume ball at Consul[xlvii] Stenborg's upstairs tomorrow night, and Torvald wants me to go as a Neapolitan fisher girl and dance the Tarantella[xlviii] because I learned that on Capri.

MRS. LINDE: Well, well— you're going to give a solo performance?

NORA: Yes, Torvald says I should. I have the costume. Torvald had it made for me in Italy, but it's so torn, and I just don't know—

MRS. LINDE: Oh, we'll soon get it fixed. Look, the trim's come loose here and there. Needle and thread?

NORA gets a sewing basket and brings it over.

Ah, we have what we need.

NORA: Kristine, this is so kind of you.

She assesses the doll and puts it in the basket to fix later.

MRS. LINDE *(sewing)*: You know— I'd like to come over for a moment tomorrow just to see you all dressed up. But I have completely forgotten to thank you for the lovely evening yesterday.

NORA gets up and walks away across the floor.

NORA: Yes, Torvald really knows how to make his home nice and pleasant.

MRS. LINDE: So do you. But tell me, is Dr. Rank always so depressed?

NORA: No, yesterday it was very noticeable. But he has a very serious disease. He has softening of the spine,[xlix] poor thing. His father was a despicable creature, who kept mistresses and such— and that's why he's been sickly since childhood.

MRS. LINDE *(lets her sewing sink to her lap)*: Nora, how do you know about such things?

NORA *(pacing; dismissively)*: Pah, when you have three children, you get help from women— women who are sort of halfway knowledgeable about medicine— and they tell you things.

MRS. LINDE *(sewing again; brief silence)*: Does Dr. Rank come here every day?

NORA: Every single day. He and Torvald have been best friends since they were young. He's *my* friend, too. Dr. Rank sort of belongs in this house.[l] He lives downstairs.

MRS. LINDE: When you introduced us yesterday, he assured me that he had often heard my name mentioned in this house— but I noticed your husband had no idea who I was. How could Dr. Rank—?

NORA: Yes, that's true. Torvald is so incredibly fond of me— he wants me all to himself, as he puts it. He used to become very jealous if I even mentioned any of my friends from home. So, of course, I stopped. But with Dr. Rank, I can always talk about things like that— he likes to listen to me.

MRS. LINDE: Listen here, Nora, you're still a child in so many ways. I am a little older,[li] and have a little more experience. You should see to it that you get out of this... this *thing* with Dr. Rank.

NORA: What kind of *thing* with Dr. Rank?

MRS. LINDE: Yesterday you talked about a rich admirer who'd give you money—

NORA: One who doesn't exist, unfortunately.

MRS. LINDE: Is Dr. Rank wealthy?

NORA: Yes, he is.

MRS. LINDE: And has no one to support?

NORA: No, nobody; but—?

MRS. LINDE: And he comes here *every single day?*

NORA: Yes, I told you he does.

MRS. LINDE: And he calls himself a gentleman.

NORA: I don't understand you at all.

MRS. LINDE: Don't pretend, Nora. Do you think I can't figure out who you've borrowed the money from?

NORA: Have you lost your mind? How can you imagine anything like that! A friend of ours, who comes here every single day! That would be a terribly awkward situation!

MRS. LINDE: So really, it wasn't him?

NORA: No, I assure you. It never occurred to me for a moment— Besides, he didn't have any money to lend at the time— he inherited it afterwards.

MRS. LINDE: Well, I think that was lucky for you.

NORA: It would never enter my mind to ask Dr. Rank— Still, I'm pretty sure that if I asked him—

MRS. LINDE: But of course you won't do *that.*

NORA: No, of course not. I can't imagine that it would be necessary. But I—

>   *(Stops)*

When you pay off all that you owe, you get the note back, right?

MRS. LINDE: Yes, of course.

NORA: And can tear it into one hundred thousand pieces and burn it up— the disgusting, filthy paper!

>   *MRS. LINDE looks at her fixedly, puts the sewing things aside*
>   *and stands up slowly.*

MRS. LINDE: Nora, you're hiding something from me.

NORA: How can you tell?

MRS. LINDE: Something has happened to you since yesterday morning. What is it?

NORA *(goes towards her)*: Kristine!

> *She listens.*

Hush! Torvald's home. Look— go and sit with the children for a moment. Torvald can't stand the sight of mending.[iii] Let Anne-Marie help you.

MRS. LINDE *(gathering some of the things)*: I'm not leaving until you tell me what's happened.

> *MRS. LINDE goes at the same moment as HELMER enters from the entry.*

NORA *(goes to meet him)*: Oh, how I've waited for you, Torvald dear.

HELMER: Was that the seamstress—?

NORA: No, it was Kristine, she's helping me mend my costume. You can't imagine how beautiful I will be.

HELMER: Yes, wasn't that a good idea I had?

NORA: Splendid!

HELMER: You're going to rehearse, I suppose.

NORA: And you're going to work?

HELMER: Yes.

> *He shows a pile of papers and moves towards his office.*

NORA: Torvald.

HELMER *(stops)*: Yes.

NORA: If your little squirrel begged you ever so sweetly for one thing—? ...Would you do it?

HELMER: I must know what it is first.

NORA: The squirrel would run around and do tricks if you said yes.

HELMER: Out with it.

NORA: I would play a fairy and dance for you in the moonlight, Torvald.

HELMER: Nora— It's not the same thing you hinted at this morning, is it?

NORA *(closer)*: Yes, Torvald, I beg you!

HELMER: You really have the stomach to drag it up again?

NORA: Yes, yes, you *must* give in to me— you *must* let Krogstad keep his position at the bank.

HELMER: My dear Nora, I've decided to give his position to Mrs. Linde.

NORA: That's enormously kind of you— but surely you can just fire somebody else.

HELMER: Unbelievable!

NORA: It's for your own sake. Krogstad writes in the nastiest newspapers— you said so yourself. He can do so much damage to you— to your reputation. I am so afraid—

HELMER: Ah, I see. You're scared of old memories.

NORA: What do you mean?

HELMER: You're thinking about your father.

NORA: Yes, yes! Remember how those evil people wrote about Papa and slandered him? It was terrible. He would've been fired if the department hadn't sent you there to investigate, and if you hadn't been so kind and helpful to him.

HELMER: There is a considerable difference between your father and me. Your father was a public servant not above reproach. But I am. And I plan to stay that way as long as I am in a position of public trust. The success of the bank depends on my reputation.

NORA: But, no one knows what evil people can invent. We could have such a good, happy and carefree home— you and me and the children, Torvald! That is why I sincerely beg you—

HELMER: The fact that you beg for him makes it impossible for me to keep him. Everyone at the bank knows I'm going to fire Krogstad. If there's a rumor that the new bank director allowed himself to be swayed by his wife—

NORA: Yes, what then—?

HELMER: I'd be a laughing stock— people would think that I am easily manipulated by all kinds of foreign influences! I have my reasons— it would be impossible to work with him.

NORA: What are they?

HELMER: I might've been able to overlook his moral shortcomings—

NORA: Yes, that's true, isn't it, Torvald?

HELMER: And he is supposed to be very good at what he does. But, he was an acquaintance of mine in law school. It was one of these hastily made friendships, which later in life embarrasses you. You might as well know— we are on a first-name basis.[liii] And Krogstad is not hiding that fact around others. The opposite in fact— he flaunts it— he persists with "Torvald, Torvald" at every opportunity. He'd make my position at the bank insufferable.[liv]

NORA: Torvald, these are only petty things.

HELMER: What do you mean? Petty? You think I am petty!

NORA: No, the opposite, dear Torvald, and because of that—

HELMER: You call my grounds for action *petty,* then I may as well be petty! Yes indeed!— Well, I will put an end to all this.

> *He goes to the door to the entry and calls.*

Helene!

NORA: What do you want?

HELMER *(looks for something in his papers)*: A decision.

HELENE enters.

See here— take this letter— get hold of a messenger and let him deliver it. Quickly. The address is on the envelope. Here's money.

HELENE: Very well.

HELENE leaves with the letter.

NORA: Torvald— what was in that letter?

HELMER: Krogstad's notice.

NORA: Get it back, Torvald!

HELMER: Nora, I forgive you this anxiety even though it is insulting to me. It is. I'm not afraid of some vindictive lawyer. I have the courage and the strength to take on anything life throws at me. I can do that for both of us—

NORA *(horrified)*: That is something you will never ever do. But, please get it back! There's still time. Do it for my sake— for your own sake— for the sake of the children! Do you hear, Torvald— do it! You don't know what this can do to us.

HELMER: Too late.

NORA: Yes, too late.

BLACKOUT.

INTERMISSION

ACT II

SCENE 1

NORA is alone on stage. She pulls herself together as DOCTOR RANK enters the room. During the following it is beginning to grow dark outside.

NORA: Good day, Dr. Rank. You mustn't go in to Torvald yet—

I think he is busy with something.

RANK: And You?

NORA (*while he enters the room and she closes the door to the entry after him*): For You, I always have some time to spare. You know that.

RANK: Thank You. I will make use of that time for as long as I can.

NORA: What do You mean by that?

RANK: Does that phrase startle You?

NORA: Well, it is a strange way of putting things. What could happen?

RANK: Exactly what I knew would happen. Still, I didn't think that it would come quite so soon.

NORA grabs his arm.

NORA: What did You find out? Dr. Rank, You must tell me!

RANK sits down by the stove.

RANK: It's all going downhill. There's nothing to be done about it.

NORA (*relieved*)[iv]: Is it You—?

RANK: Who else? It can't do any good to lie to myself. I am the most miserable of all my patients, Mrs. Helmer. I've just undertaken a final assessment of my internal accounts. Bankrupt. Within a month I'll probably be rotting up there in the cemetery.

NORA: O shame, what ugly things You say.

RANK: This *is* damned ugly. The worst thing is there will be so much more ugliness before it's over. There is only one examination left— when I'm done with that, I'll know approximately when the final disintegration will begin. There is something I want to ask You. Helmer has a delicate nature, he can't stand anything ugly. I don't want him to come to my sickroom—

NORA: Oh but Dr. Rank—

RANK: I don't want to hav'im there. In no way. I will close my door to him— As soon as I have complete certainty about the worst, I'll send You my visiting card with a black cross on it. Then You'll know the devastation[vi] has begun.

NORA: You are certainly impossible today. And I was so hoping You'd be in a really good mood.

RANK: With death at hand?— And to do penance for someone else's guilt. Is there any justice in that? In every single family, some kind of retribution is exacted for—[lvii]

NORA *(holding her hands over her ears)*: Nonsense! Cheer up, cheer up![lviii]

RANK: Yes, I suppose there's nothing to do but laugh. My poor, innocent spine must suffer for my father's "happy" lieutenant days.[lix]

NORA *(by the table)*: He was so addicted to asparagus and *paté de fois gras*. Wasn't that so?

RANK: Yes, and to truffles.

NORA: Yes truffles, yes. And to oysters, I believe?

RANK: Yes oysters, oysters, of course.

NORA: And all that port and champagne. It is sad that all these delicious things must attack your bones.

RANK: Especially when they attack unfortunate bones, bones that never had a chance to enjoy them.

NORA: Oh yes, that is the saddest of all.

RANK *(looks searchingly at her)*: Hm—

NORA *(after a moment)*: Why did You smile?

RANK: No, it was You who grinned.

NORA: No, it was You, who smiled, Dr. Rank!

RANK: I think You're a bigger rogue than I had realized.

NORA: I am primed for mad things today.

RANK: So it seems.

NORA *(with both hands on his shoulders)*: Dear, dear Dr. Rank, You will not die and leave Torvald and me.

RANK: Oh, You'll easily get over the loss. One who passes on is soon forgotten.

NORA *(looks at him fearfully)*: Do You believe that?

RANK: Both You and Helmer will forge new friendships when I am gone. You're already well on Your way it seems. What was this Mrs. Linde doing here last night?

NORA: Aha— but You can't be jealous of poor Kristine?

RANK: Yes, I am. She will become my successor here in this house. When I've expired, perhaps this female[lx] will—

NORA: Shhh, don't speak so loudly, she's in there.

RANK: Again today? There You see.

NORA: Only to mend my costume. My God, how unreasonable You are.

She sits down on the sofa.

Now be good, Dr. Rank— tomorrow You'll see how beautifully I dance— and You'll imagine that I am doing it only for You— yes, and of course for Torvald too.

She takes several things out of the box.

Dr. Rank— sit there, I want to show You something.

RANK *(sits down)*: What is it?

NORA: Look here. Look!

RANK: Silk stockings.

NORA: Flesh colored.[lxi] Aren't these gorgeous? Yes, It's too dark in here now, but tomorrow— No, no, no, You may only see the foot. Ah well, You might as well get to see the upper part too.

RANK: Hm—

NORA: Why do You look so critical? Do You think they won't fit?

RANK: I cannot possibly have any opinion about that.

NORA *(looks at him for a moment)*: Shame on You.

She gently strikes him over the ear with the stockings.

That's what You deserve.

NORA packs the stockings up again.

RANK: And what other wonders will I get to see.

NORA: You won't get to see a smidgeon more— because You're being naughty.

NORA hums a little and looks through the things in the box.

RANK *(after a brief silence)*: When I am here, like this, together with You, I can't fathom— what would've happened to me if I had never come here— to this house.

More softly, looking straight ahead at something.

And to have to leave it all—

NORA: Nonsense, You won't leave it.

RANK *(as before)*: —and not to be able to leave behind even a poor sign of gratitude— barely a fleeting regret— nothing but an empty space, which can be filled by whoever shows up first.

NORA: And if I asked You now for—? No—

RANK: For what?

NORA: For a great proof of Your friendship—

RANK: Yes, yes?

NORA: No I mean— for an enormous favor—

RANK: Would You really, for once, make me so happy?

NORA: You don't know what it is.

RANK: Well then, tell me.

NORA: No I can't, Dr. Rank. It's something so unreasonably big— some advice and help and a favor—

RANK: All the better. I can't fathom what You mean. Tell me. Don't You trust me?

NORA: Yes, like no one else. You are my truest and best friend. So, I want to tell You. There is something You can help me to prevent. You know how dearly, how deeply Torvald loves me, he would never hesitate to give his life for my sake.[lxii]

RANK (*leaning toward her*): Nora,[lxiii]— do You really think that he is the only one who—?

NORA (*with a light jerk*): Who—?

RANK: Who would gladly give his life for Your sake.

NORA (*heavily*): Yes, well.

RANK: I swore to myself that You should know before the end. I'll never find a better opportunity— Yes, Nora, now You know. And now You know that You can confide in me.

NORA (*gets up; evenly and calmly*): Let me—

> RANK *makes space for her to pass but remains sitting.*

RANK: Nora—

NORA (*in the doorway to the entry*): Helene, bring in the lamp—

> She goes over toward the stove.

Oh, dear Dr. Rank, this was badly done of You.

> He gets up.

RANK: That I love You as deeply as anyone else? That was badly done?

NORA: No, but that You went ahead and said it. That wasn't at all necessary—

RANK: What do You mean? Then, did You know all along—?

> HELENE *comes in with the lamp, puts it on the table and goes out again.*

Nora— Mrs. Helmer—[lxiv] I ask You, have You known all along?

NORA: Oh, what do I know— what I did or didn't know? I really cannot tell You— That You could be so clumsy, Dr. Rank! Everything was so pleasant.

RANK: Well, in any case, You now have assurance that I stand ready to advise You with body and soul. Will You please tell me.

NORA (*looks at him*): After this?

RANK: I beg You, let me know what it is.

NORA: You can know nothing now.

RANK: Don't punish me like this. Allow me to do whatever is humanly possible.

NORA: You can do nothing for me— Besides I really don't need any help. It's just my imagination. Yes, of course!

> She sits down in the rocker, looks at him, smiles.

Well, You are certainly a fine gentleman, Dr. Rank. Aren't You a little ashamed now that the lamp is lit?

RANK: No, actually not. But maybe I should leave? Forever.

NORA: No, You'll come here as before. You know very well that Torvald can't be without You.

RANK: And *You*?

NORA: Oh, I always think it is tremendously pleasant when You are here.

RANK: That is precisely what lured me onto the wrong track. You are an enigma to me. There were times I thought You'd almost rather be with me than with Helmer.

NORA: Yes, you see, there are some people you love best, and others you'd rather *be* with.

RANK: Oh yes.

NORA: When I was at home, I loved Papa best. But I always thought it was enormous fun to sneak down to the maids' room— because they never lectured me— to hear them talk and laugh among themselves.

RANK: Aha, I've replaced the maids.

> NORA jumps up and over to him.

NORA: My dear, kind Dr. Rank, I didn't mean it like that. But You can see, can't You, Torvald is like Papa—

> HELENE comes in from the entry.

HELENE: Madam!

> Whispers and hands NORA a visiting card.

NORA (glances at the card): Ah!

> Puts it in her pocket.

RANK: Something wrong?[lxv]

NORA: No, no, not at all. It's only some— it's my costume—

RANK: Isn't that Your costume?

NORA: Oh, yes that one, but this is another one I've ordered. Torvald mustn't know I—

RANK: Aha, there we have the big secret.

NORA: Yes exactly. Go in to him, he is sitting in his office, keep him busy for a while—

RANK: Rest assured, he will not get away from me.

RANK goes into Helmer's office.

NORA *(to Helene)*: And he is standing there waiting in the kitchen?

HELENE: Yes, he came up the back stairs—

NORA: Didn't you tell him that there was someone here?

HELENE: Yes, but it didn't help.

NORA: He won't leave?

HELENE: No, he won't leave until he gets to talk to the Mrs.

NORA: Then let him come in, but quietly. Helene, you must not tell anyone. It's a surprise for my husband.

HELENE: Yes, Yes, I understand.

HELENE leaves. NORA goes over and bolts the door to Helmer's office.

NORA: It cannot happen. It must not happen.

HELENE returns with Lawyer[lxvi] KROGSTAD, then exits. He is dressed in travelling clothes, outer boots and leather cap.[lxvii]

NORA approaches him.

Keep Your voice down, my husband is home.

KROGSTAD: It doesn't matter.

NORA: What do You want with me?

KROGSTAD: Answers.

NORA: Then hurry up. What is it?

KROGSTAD: I suppose You know I received my notice.

NORA: I couldn't prevent it, Mr. Krogstad. I fought to the utmost of my ability on Your behalf, but it didn't help.

KROGSTAD: Doesn't Your husband love you at all? He knows what I can do to You, and he dares—

NORA: How can You think I've told him?

KROGSTAD: Oh no, I didn't think You had. It's not like my good Torvald Helmer to show so much manly courage—

NORA: Mr. Krogstad, I demand respect for my husband.

KROGSTAD: Goodness, all due respect. But since You're keeping our business anxiously hidden from him, I assume You now have a clearer understanding of what You've actually done?

NORA: What do You want with me?

KROGSTAD: I wanted to see how You are doing, Mrs. Helmer. I've been thinking about You all day. Even a debt collector, a shady lawyer, a hack journalist, a— well, someone like me— has a little thing called a tender heart.

NORA: Then show it, think of my small children.

KROGSTAD: Have You and Your husband thought of mine? Doesn't matter.

I will not bring a case against You immediately. The whole thing can be settled amicably, it doesn't need to be made public. It will remain between the three of us.

NORA: My husband must never know about any of this.

KROGSTAD: How will You prevent that? Can You pay off the entire debt?

NORA: No, not right away.

KROGSTAD: Or do You have some way of raising money in the next few days?

NORA: No way that I'd care to.

KROGSTAD: Well, that wouldn't help You anyway. If You were standing here with large amounts of cash— You still couldn't pry the note from my hands.

NORA: What are you going to do with it?

KROGSTAD: I just want to keep it— have it in my possession. No outsider will get wind of it.

If You happen to be considering doing something desperate or—

Silence from NORA.

—if You are thinking of running away from home—

More silence.

—or if You are thinking of something even worse—

NORA: How can You know that?

KROGSTAD: —then You need to forget about that.

NORA: How can You know that I am thinking of *that*?

KROGSTAD: Most of us think of that to begin with. I considered it, but honestly, I didn't have the courage—

NORA *(under her breath)*: I don't either.

KROGSTAD *(relieved)*: You don't either?

NORA: I don't.

KROGSTAD: It would be a very stupid thing to do. As soon as the first domestic storm has blown over— I have a letter, here in my pocket, to Your husband—

NORA: And it says everything?

KROGSTAD: As gently put as possible.

NORA *(quickly)*: Tear it to pieces. Let me know how much You're demanding from my husband and I'll get it.

KROGSTAD: I don't want money from Your husband.

NORA: What do You want then?

KROGSTAD: I want to stand on my own feet again, Mrs. Helmer. I want to move up, and Your husband will help me do that. For a year and a half I have not been guilty of anything dishonorable— all that time I have struggled under dire circumstances. It was enough for me to work my way up, step by step. Now I am discarded— thrown away! I won't be satisfied with my old position. I want advancement. I want to be back at the bank— but in a higher position. Your husband will create that for me—

NORA: He'll never do that!

KROGSTAD: He will do it, I know him, he won't dare say a word. Once I am there— You'll see! Within one year I will be the director's right hand. It will be Nils Krogstad, not Torvald Helmer, who leads the Stock Bank.

NORA: You'll never live to see that—! I have the courage to do it now.

KROGSTAD: You are not going to— A fine fastidious lady like Yourself—

NORA: You'll see, You'll see!

KROGSTAD: Under the ice, perhaps? Down in the cold, coal black water? Floating up in the spring, ugly, unrecognizable, bloated, with your hair fallen off—

NORA: You can't scare me.

KROGSTAD: You can't scare me either. People don't do such things, Mrs. Helmer. Besides, what good would it do? Are You forgetting that I will control what they'll say about you after You're dead?

NORA stands speechless and looks at him.

Don't do anything stupid. When Helmer receives my letter I'll expect a message from him. Remember it's Your husband who has forced me down this path. I will never forgive him for that. Goodbye, Mrs. Helmer.

KROGSTAD goes out through the entry. NORA moves toward the door to the entry, opens it a crack and listens.

NORA: Leaving. Doesn't drop the letter. Oh no, no, of course that would be impossible!

She opens the door more and more.

What? He's not walking downstairs. Is he having second thoughts—?

A letter falls in the mailbox. KROGSTAD's steps are heard descending the stairs.

With a stifled scream, NORA runs across the floor and toward the sofa table, brief pause.

It's in the mailbox.

Frightened, she sneaks over to the door to the entry.

There it is— Torvald, Torvald— now we are lost!

MRS. LINDE *(in with the Tarantella costume)*: All mended. Should we try it on—?

> *She throws the dress on the sofa.*

What's wrong? You look upset.

NORA: Come here. Do you see that letter? *There—*

> *She points to the mailbox off.*

MRS. LINDE: Yes, yes, I see it.

NORA: It's from Krogstad—

MRS. LINDE: Nora— Krogstad lent you the money!

NORA: Yes— and now Torvald will know everything.

MRS. LINDE: Ah, believe me, Nora, it's for the best.

NORA: There is more I didn't tell you. I forged a signature—

MRS. LINDE: For heaven's sake—?

NORA: I only want to say this Kristine— you must be my witness.

MRS. LINDE: Witness? What must I—?

NORA: If there should be someone, who wanted to take it all on himself[lxviii] the whole burden, all the blame, you understand—

MRS. LINDE: Yes, yes, but how can you think—?

NORA: Then you must bear witness that it is not true, Kristine. I am not insane— I know perfectly well what I am doing— and I say to you: no one else knew about it. I alone did it. Remember that.

MRS. LINDE: I will. But I don't understand.

NORA: Oh, how would you be able to understand? Because now the wonderful thing will happen.

MRS. LINDE: The wonderful thing?

NORA: Yes, the wonderful thing. But it is so horrible, Kristine— it *must* not happen.

MRS. LINDE: I'll go and talk to Krogstad right away.

NORA: Don't go, he is dangerous!

MRS. LINDE: There was a time when he would gladly have done anything for me.

NORA: What?

MRS. LINDE: Where does he live?

NORA: Oh, how would I know—? Oh yes,

> *She sticks her hand into her pocket.*

here's his card. But the letter, the letter—!

HELMER *(in his office)*: Nora!

NORA *(screams in fear)*: Oh, what is it? What do you want?

HELMER: Well, well, don't get so alarmed. We're not coming in. You've locked the door, are you trying on your costume?

NORA: Yes, yes, I'm trying it on. I will look so lovely, Torvald.

MRS. LINDE *(who has been reading the card)*: He lives right around the corner!

NORA: Yes, but that doesn't help. We are lost. The letter's in the mailbox.

MRS. LINDE: And your husband has the only key?

NORA: Yes.

MRS. LINDE: Krogstad could demand his letter back unread, he could invent an excuse—

NORA: But Torvald usually checks the mailbox around this time—

MRS. LINDE: Delay it— go talk to him. I'll be back as soon as I can.

> *MRS. LINDE leaves quickly through the door to the entry.*
> *NORA goes over to the door to Helmer's office, unbolts it and*
> *peers in.*

NORA: Torvald!

HELMER *(in the office)*: Well, I'm finally allowed back into my own living room? Come, Rank, now we'll get to see—

> *(In the doorway)*

But what's this?

NORA: What, Torvald dear?

HELMER: Rank prepared me for some magnificent costume surprise.

RANK *(in the doorway)*: I— That's what I thought, but clearly I was mistaken.

NORA: Yes, no one will be allowed to admire me in my full splendor until tomorrow.

HELMER: Nora, dear, you look strained. Have you been rehearsing too much?

NORA: No. I can't get anywhere without your help. I have completely forgotten everything.

HELMER: Oh, we'll soon refresh your memory.

NORA: Yes, take me under your wing, Torvald. Promise me that? Oh, I am so anxious. The big party— You must devote yourself completely to me this evening. Not an ounce of business— What do you say, Torvald, dear?

HELMER: I promise, this evening I will be completely at your service— you helpless little thing—

> *He goes toward the door to the entry.*

NORA: What do you need out there?

HELMER: I want to see if there is any mail.

NORA: No, no, don't do that, Torvald!

HELMER: Just let me check.

> *NORA at the piano, beats out the first measures of the tarantella.[lxix]*

> *(At the door, stops)*

Aha!

NORA: I can't dance tomorrow if I don't rehearse with you.

HELMER *(goes over to her)*: Nora, are you really so nervous?

NORA: Yes, enormously nervous. Let's rehearse right now, there's still time before dinner. Oh sit down and play for me, Torvald— correct me— guide me.

HELMER: With pleasure, with great pleasure, since you wish it.

> *He sits down at the piano. NORA grabs the tambourine out of the box and also a long colorful shawl, with which, quick as lightning, she wraps herself. She steps out on the floor with one jump and calls out.*

NORA: Play for me! I want to dance!

> *HELMER plays. NORA dances. DR. RANK stands next to the piano behind HELMER and looks on.*

HELMER *(playing)*: Slower— slower.

NORA: Can't help it.

HELMER: Not so violent, Nora!

NORA: It must be just like this.

HELMER *(stops)*: No, no, this won't do at all.

NORA *(smiles and waves the tambourine)*: Wasn't that what I was telling you?

RANK: Let me play for her.

HELMER: Yes do, then I can direct her.

> *RANK sits down at the piano and plays; NORA dances with increasing wildness. HELMER has placed himself by the stove and regularly addresses correcting remarks to her during the dance; she does not seem to hear them; her hair loosens and falls down over her shoulders; she does not stop to put it up but continues to dance.*

> *MRS. LINDE comes in and stands speechless in the doorway.*

MRS. LINDE: Ah—!

NORA *(while dancing)*: See the fun and games, Kristine!

HELMER: Nora, you're dancing as if your life depended on it.

NORA: It does.

HELMER: Rank, stop, this is just pure madness. Stop.

> *RANK stops playing and NORA suddenly stands still.*

HELMER (CONT'D) *(over to her)*: Unbelievable. You've forgotten everything I have taught you.

NORA tosses the tambourine away from her.

NORA: I told you. You must rehearse me up to the last moment. Do you promise, Torvald?

HELMER: You can count on it.

NORA: You will not think of anything but me— you will not open any letter— not open the mailbox—

HELMER: Nora, I can see it in your face. There's a letter from that person.

NORA: I don't know— I think so— but don't read it now— nothing ugly must come between us until everything is over.

RANK *(softly to Helmer)*: You shouldn't contradict her.[lxx]

HELMER wraps one arm around her.

HELMER: The child will have her wish. But tomorrow night, after you have danced, then—

NORA: Then you are free.

HELENE *(in the doorway to the dining room)*: Ma'am, the table is set.

NORA: We will have champagne, Helene.

HELENE: Very well, Ma'am.

Goes out.

HELMER: Well well, what's this?— a feast?

NORA: Champagne-feast till dawn.

(Calls out)

And macaroons, Helene, lots of them— for once.

HELMER *(takes her hands)*: Why so wild? Now, be my little lark, like you usually are.

NORA: Oh yes, I will. But go in, and Dr. Rank, You too. Kristine, will you help me put up my hair.

RANK *(softly while they are leaving)*: There isn't anything— she isn't expecting, is she?

HELMER *(as they leave)*: Oh no, my dear Rank. It's simply the childish anxiety that I told you about.[lxxi]

NORA: Well?!

MRS. LINDE: Gone to the country. He'll be back tomorrow night. I wrote him a note.

NORA: You should've let that be. You mustn't prevent anything. Deep down it is a great joy— this— here— waiting for the wonderful thing.

MRS. LINDE: What are you waiting for?

NORA: Oh, you won't understand. Go in to them. I'll be there in a moment.

> *MRS. LINDE goes. NORA stands for a moment as if to collect herself; then she looks at her watch.[lxxii]*

Five. Seven hours to midnight. Then twenty-four hours to next midnight. Then the Tarantella will be done. Twenty-four and seven? Thirty-one hours to live.

HELMER *(in the doorway to the dining room)*: But whatever happened to my little songbird?

NORA *(towards him with open arms)*: Here she is!

ACT II, SCENE 2

The same room. The sofa table, with chairs around it, has been moved out into the middle of the floor. A lamp is lit on the table. The door to the entry is open. Dance music is heard from the floor above.

MRS. LINDE is sitting at the table putting in the final stitches on Emmy's doll. Her knitting lies untouched on another table. She doesn't seem to be able to concentrate. She gets up a couple of times and listens tensely for the apartment door. She occasionally looks at her watch. She goes out into the entry and cautiously opens the apartment door; quiet steps are heard on the stairs; she whispers.

MRS. LINDE *(entering)*: Come in. No one is here.

KROGSTAD *(in the doorway)*: I got Your note.[lxxiii] What does it mean?

MRS. LINDE: I need to talk to You.

KROGSTAD: Here? In this house?

MRS. LINDE: It's impossible at the boarding-house— my room has no private entrance. Come in, we're alone. The maid is asleep and the Helmers are at a party upstairs.

KROGSTAD: The Helmers are dancing this evening? Really?

MRS. LINDE: Yes, why wouldn't they?

KROGSTAD: True enough— why wouldn't they?

MRS. LINDE: Krogstad. Let's talk.

KROGSTAD: Do we have anything more to talk about?

MRS. LINDE: We have a great deal to talk about.

KROGSTAD: I didn't think so.

MRS. LINDE: No, because You never fully understood me.

KROGSTAD: What was there to understand? It happens every day— a heartless woman sends a man packing as soon as she gets a better offer.

MRS. LINDE: Do You think that I am so completely heartless? Do You think it was easy for me to break things off with You?

KROGSTAD: Wasn't it?

MRS. LINDE: Krogstad, You've really believed that?

KROGSTAD: Then why did You write me the way You did?

MRS. LINDE: What else could I do? When I broke it off with You— I felt it was my duty to destroy all the feelings You had for me.

KROGSTAD *(clenches his fists)*: So, that's why. And this— all for money!

MRS. LINDE: Remember, I had a helpless mother and two small brothers. We couldn't wait for You, Krogstad— Your prospects were so uncertain.

KROGSTAD: Maybe— but You didn't have the right to reject me for someone else.

MRS. LINDE: Yes— I don't know. I have asked myself many times if I had the right to do that.

KROGSTAD *(more softly)*: When I lost You, it was as if all solid ground slipped away from under my feet. Look at me now— I'm shipwrecked— I'm a man adrift on a wreck.

MRS. LINDE: Help is close.

KROGSTAD: It was close— then You got in the way.

MRS. LINDE: I didn't know. I only heard today that I'm Your replacement at the bank.

KROGSTAD *(looking at her, searching)*: I believe You. But now that You know, won't You step aside?

MRS. LINDE: No— because it wouldn't benefit You at all.

KROGSTAD: Benefit, benefit— I would do it.

MRS. LINDE: I've learned to act sensibly. Life and hard bitter necessity have taught me that.

KROGSTAD: And life has taught me not to believe in platitudes.

MRS. LINDE: Then life has taught You a very sensible thing. But You still believe in actions?

KROGSTAD: What do You mean?

MRS. LINDE: You said that You're standing like a shipwrecked man adrift on a wreck.

KROGSTAD: I have good reason to say that.

MRS. LINDE: I'm like a shipwrecked woman clinging to a wreck. No one to mourn, no one to care for.

KROGSTAD: That was Your choice.

MRS. LINDE: At that time, I had no other choice.

KROGSTAD: So?

MRS. LINDE: Krogstad, if we two shipwrecked human beings could reach for each other.

KROGSTAD: What are You saying?

MRS. LINDE: Two on one wreck can survive better than each drifting alone.

KROGSTAD: Kristine![lxxiv]

MRS. LINDE: Why do You think I came to town?

KROGSTAD: You were thinking about me?

MRS. LINDE: I must work if I am to endure life. All my life I have worked, and it has been my best and only joy. But now I am standing alone in the world, empty and forsaken. To work for yourself, there is no joy in that. Krogstad, give me somebody and something to work for.

KROGSTAD: I don't believe this. It's nothing other than self-sacrificing, hysterical female pride.

MRS. LINDE: Have You ever known me to be hysterical?

KROGSTAD: Could You really do this? Tell me— You know all about my past?

MRS. LINDE: Yes.

KROGSTAD: And You know about my reputation?

MRS. LINDE: Just now You sounded like You thought You could've been a different person with me.

KROGSTAD: Yes.

MRS. LINDE: Couldn't that still happen?

KROGSTAD: Kristine— You are serious? Yes, You are. I can see it in Your eyes. You really have the courage—?

MRS. LINDE: I need someone to be a mother to— and Your children need a mother. We need each other. Krogstad, I have faith in You— who You are— I can face anything with You.

KROGSTAD grips her with both hands.

KROGSTAD: Thank You, thank You, Kristine— Ah, but I forgot—

MRS. LINDE *(listens)*: Shh! The tarantella! Go, go!

KROGSTAD: Why? What is it?

MRS. LINDE: Do You hear that dance upstairs? When it is over, they'll be back down.

KROGSTAD: Oh yes, I'll go. It's all pointless anyway— You don't know what I've done to the Helmers.

MRS. LINDE: Yes, Krogstad, I know.

KROGSTAD: And still You have the courage to—?

MRS. LINDE: I understand where desperation can push a man like You.

KROGSTAD: If only I can undo what I have done.

MRS. LINDE: You could, I think— Your letter is still in the mailbox.

KROGSTAD *(looks at her searchingly)*: So that's it? You want to save Your friend. Just say it— Tell me straight. Is that it?

MRS. LINDE: A woman who has sold herself for the sake of others does not do it again.

KROGSTAD: I'll ask for my letter back.

MRS. LINDE: No, no.

KROGSTAD: Yes of course. I'll wait here until the Helmers come down. I'll tell him that he must give it back— that it's only about being fired— that he shouldn't read it—

MRS. LINDE: No, Krogstad, Don't ask for it back.

KROGSTAD: Wasn't that why You wanted to see me?

MRS. LINDE: Yes, at first, but I have witnessed unbelievable things in this house. Helmer must know everything, this unfortunate secret must be brought to light. Go, go! The dance is over, we aren't safe a moment longer.

KROGSTAD: I will wait for You downstairs.

MRS. LINDE: Yes, do. You may walk me home.[lxxv]

KROGSTAD: I have never been this unbelievably happy.

> *KROGSTAD goes out through the apartment door, the door between the living room and the entry remains open during the following. MRS. LINDE straightens things a little, props the doll up by the lamp for Nora to see and places her outerwear in readiness.*

> *HELMER's and NORA's voices are heard outside. A key is turned and Helmer leads Nora almost by force through the apartment door into the entry. She is dressed in the Italian costume with a big black shawl thrown over her; he is in black evening wear with an open black domino[lxxvi] over it.*

NORA *(in the doorway to the entry, resisting)*: No, no, no— not in here! I want to go back upstairs. I don't want to leave so early.

HELMER: But dearest Nora—

NORA: Oh I beg you, I implore you, Torvald. I beg you with all my heart— one more hour!

HELMER: Not a single minute, my sweet. We had an agreement. There now, get in the room. You'll catch a cold standing out there.

> *HELMER leads her, in spite of her resistance, gently into the room.*

MRS. LINDE: Good evening.

NORA: Kristine!

HELMER: What, Mrs. Linde, here this late?

MRS. LINDE: Yes, excuse me. I wanted to see Nora in her costume but you had already gone upstairs.

I couldn't leave without seeing her.

> *HELMER takes off NORA's shawl.*

HELMER: Take a good look at her. Isn't she lovely, Mrs. Linde?

MRS. LINDE: Yes, I must say—

HELMER: Isn't she remarkably lovely? That was the general consensus upstairs. But terribly obstinate— the sweet little thing. What will we do about that? Imagine, Mrs. Linde, I almost had to use force to get her to leave.

NORA: Oh Torvald, you'll regret that you didn't let me stay just another half hour.

HELMER: Hear for yourself, Mrs. Linde. Nora dances the tarantella— thunderous applause— which was well deserved— although there was perhaps a little too much nature in the execution. The main thing is— she is successful, tremendously successful. How could I let her stay after that? Weaken the effect? No thanks, I took my lovely little Capri girl— capricious little Capri girl— under the arm, a quick sweep around the room,[lxxvii] a bow to all sides, and— as they say in the novels— "the beautiful apparition vanished." An exit must always be effective, Mrs. Linde, I can't seem to make Nora understand that. Phew, it's warm in here.

> *Throws the domino on a chair and opens the door to his room.*

What? It's dark. Oh yes, of course. Excuse me—

> *HELMER goes in to his office and lights a couple of lamps.*

NORA *(whispers quickly and breathlessly)*: Well?!

MRS. LINDE: Nora— You must tell your husband everything.

NORA *(tonelessly)*: I knew it.

MRS. LINDE: You have nothing to fear from Krogstad but you must tell your husband.

NORA: I will not.

MRS. LINDE: Then the letter will.

NORA: Thank you, Kristine. Now I know what I must do.

> *She spots the doll, smiles, picks it up.*

Shh—!

> *HELMER comes in again.*

HELMER: Well, Mrs. Linde, are you done admiring her?

MRS. LINDE: Yes, and now I will say goodnight.

HELMER: Oh what, already?

> *MRS. LINDE smiles, turns to go.*

Is that knitting Yours?[lxxviii]

> *MRS. LINDE picks up her knitting, puts it in her bag.*

MRS. LINDE: Yes, thank You. I almost forgot it.

HELMER: Knitting is simply ugly.

> *He demonstrates briefly.*

HELMER (CONT'D): You should embroider— Ah, that was really a marvelous champagne they served.

MRS. LINDE: Goodnight, Nora, and don't be obstinate any more.

HELMER: Well spoken, Mrs. Linde!

MRS. LINDE: Goodnight, Mr. Director.

HELMER accompanies her to the apartment door.

HELMER: Goodnight, goodnight; You'll get home all right, I hope? I'd like to see You home[lxxix]— but it's not very far. Goodnight, goodnight.

MRS. LINDE goes; he locks after her and comes back in again.

Finally! She's a terrible bore.

NORA *(still holding doll):* Are you tired, Torvald?

HELMER: Not at all. I feel enormously invigorated. You? You really look tired.

NORA: Yes, but I'll soon sleep.

Kisses the doll and lays it back on the table.

HELMER: But did you notice how lively Rank was tonight?

NORA: Oh? Was he?[lxxx] I didn't get to speak with him.

HELMER: I almost didn't either. I haven't seen him in such a good mood in a long time.

Looks at her for a while; then he comes closer.

Hm— it is wonderful, though, to be home, to be alone with you—

NORA: Don't look at me like that, Torvald!

HELMER: Can't I look at my dearest possession? At all the loveliness that is mine, mine alone, mine completely.

NORA goes over to the other side of the table.

NORA: You can't speak like that to me tonight.

HELMER *(follows her):* I see, you still have the Tarantella in your blood. It makes you all the more alluring. Listen! The guests are starting to leave.

(More softly)

Nora— soon the whole house will be quiet.

NORA: Yes, I hope so.

HELMER: Yes, You do, don't you, my own darling Nora? Oh, do you know— when I am out with you— do you know why I speak so little to you, keep so far away from you, only send you a stolen glance now and then— do you know why I do that? Because then I imagine that you are my secret lover, and no one suspects there is anything between us.

NORA: Oh yes, yes, yes, I know you are thinking only about me.

HELMER: And when we are leaving, and I drape the shawl around your beautiful youthful shoulders— around this wonderful curve of the neck— I imagine you are my young bride, that we have just come from our wedding, and for the first time I am bringing you into my home— for the first time I am alone with you— quite alone with you, your young trembling—! This whole evening I have only desired you. When I saw you dance the Tarantella— enticing, luring, promising— my blood boiled. I couldn't stand it any longer— that was why I brought you home so early—

NORA: Torvald—

> There is knocking at the apartment door.

> *(Shrinks)*

Did you hear—?

HELMER: Who is it?

RANK *(outside)*: Me. Dare I come in for a moment?

HELMER *(softly, annoyed)*: Oh what does he want now?

> *(Loudly)*

Just a moment *Doctor Medicinae* Rank.[lxxxi].

> *Goes out into the entry and opens the apartment door.*

Well, it's nice of you to stop by on your way down.[lxxxii]

RANK: I thought I heard your voice and realized I wanted to look in.

> *He lets his eye quickly glide around the room.*

Ah yes, these dear familiar haunts. You two have a cozy and pleasant little nest.

HELMER: You had a pleasant time upstairs.

RANK: Splendid. Why shouldn't I? Why shouldn't I embrace everything in this world? As much as I can, and for as long as I can. The wine was excellent—

HELMER: Especially the champagne.

RANK: You noticed that too? It was unbelievable how much I could imbibe. Well, why shouldn't I have a wonderful evening after a day well spent?

NORA: Doctor Rank, I believe You undertook a scientific examination today.

RANK: I did!

HELMER: Well! Little Nora is talking about scientific examinations!

NORA: Dare I wish You good luck with the result?

RANK: Yes indeed, You may.

NORA: It was good then?

RANK: The best possible for the physician and the patient— certainty.

NORA *(quickly and searchingly)*: Certainty?

RANK: Complete certainty. So shouldn't I have a wonderful evening after that?

NORA: Yes, You should.

HELMER: I say so too. Just don't end up paying for it tomorrow.

RANK: Well, as you know you don't get anything in life for free.

NORA: Dr. Rank— What should You and I be at the next masquerade?

RANK: You and I? I'll tell You. You will be a Child of Good Luck—

HELMER: Yes, but come up with a costume that can signify *that.*

RANK: Let your wife come just as she is— *som hun står og går—*

HELMER: That was aptly put. But, what will you be?

RANK: My dear friend, at the next masquerade I will be invisible.

HELMER: That's a funny idea.

RANK: There is a big black hat— haven't you heard about the invisibility hat? It is put on you, and then no one in the world can see you.

HELMER *(with a suppressed smile)*: No, you're right.

RANK: But I am forgetting what I came here for. Helmer, give me a cigar, one of the dark Havanas.

HELMER: With great pleasure.

> He offers him the cigar box. RANK takes one and cuts off the tip.

RANK: Thanks.

> NORA strikes a wax match.[lxxxiii]

NORA: Let me give You a light.

RANK: Thank you.

> She holds the match for him; he lights the cigar.

And so, Goodbye![lxxxiv]

HELMER: Goodnight, Goodnight, dear friend!

NORA: Sleep well, Dr. Rank.

RANK: Thanks for that wish.

NORA: Wish me the same.

RANK: You? Well then, since You want it— Sleep well. And thanks for the light.

> Nods to the two of them and leaves.

HELMER *(subdued)*: He's had a lot to drink.

NORA *(absentminded)*: Maybe so.

> HELMER takes his key chain out of his pocket and goes out into the entry.

Torvald— what are you doing?

HELMER: I need to empty the mailbox, it's full, there won't be space for the newspapers tomorrow morning—

NORA: Are you going to work tonight?

HELMER: You know I'm not— What's this? Someone's been at the lock.

NORA: At the lock—?

HELMER: Yes. Who could—? I'd never believe that the maids[lxxxv]—? There's a broken hairpin. Nora, it's yours—

NORA *(quick)*: It must be the children—

HELMER: You must break them of that... behavior. Hm, hm— well, I got it opened anyway.

> *He takes out the contents of the mail box, comes back into the room and closes the door to the entry.*

See how it's piled up.

> *(Leafs through them)*

What on earth is this? Two visiting cards— from Rank.[lxxxvi] He must have stuck them in when he left. This is really gruesome. Look— There is a black cross above the name. It's as if he were announcing his own death.

NORA: He is.

HELMER: What? Do you know something I don't? Has he told you something?

NORA: Yes. When that card arrives, it's his final goodbye. He wants to lock himself in and die.

HELMER: My poor friend. I knew that I wouldn't be allowed to keep him for long. But so soon— And he hides himself away to die like a wounded animal.

NORA: If it must happen, Torvald, then it's best it happens without words, don't you agree?

HELMER *(paces back and forth)*: He had become so much a part of us. I don't think I can imagine him gone. His suffering, his loneliness was like a cloudy backdrop to our sunlit happiness. Maybe it's best like this. For him.

> *He stops.*

And for us, Nora. Now we only have each other.

> *He throws his arms around her.*

I don't think I can hold you tight enough. Do you know, Nora— I often wish that an impending danger would threaten you, so I could risk life and limb and everything, everything, for your sake.

> *NORA tears herself loose and says, strongly and determinedly:*

NORA: Read your letters now, Torvald.

HELMER: No, no, not tonight. I want to be with you—

NORA: With the thought of your friend's death—

HELMER: You're right. We're both shaken by it— something ugly has come between us— thoughts of death and decomposition.[lxxxvii] We need to free ourselves from these thoughts.

NORA *(hanging around his neck):* Torvald— good night! Good night!

>   *HELMER kisses her on the forehead.*

HELMER: Good night, my little songbird. Sleep well, Nora.

>   *HELMER goes with the packet of letters into his room and closes the door after him.*

>   *NORA with wild eyes, staggers around, grabs Helmer's domino,[lxxxviii] flings it around herself, her movement not slow or gentle, and whispers quickly, hoarsely and in short bursts.*

NORA: Never see him again. Never. Never. Never.

>   *Throws her shawl over her head, sees the doll, touches it but does not pick it up.*

Never see the children again either— Oh, the ice cold black water. Oh, the bottomless— this— Oh if it were only over and done with— He has it. He is reading it. Oh no, no— not yet. Torvald, goodbye to you and the children—[lxxxix]

>   *She wants to dash out through the door to the entry; at the same moment HELMER throws open his door and stands there with an opened letter in his hand.*

HELMER: Nora!

NORA *(catches herself in mid-scream):* Ah—!

HELMER: Do you know what this letter says?

NORA: Yes, I know what it says. Let me go! Let me out!

HELMER *(holds her back):* Where do you plan to go?

NORA *(tries to tear herself loose):* You must not save me, Torvald!

HELMER *(whirls back):* True! It's true what he writes? Horrible! No, no— it's impossible that this could be true.

NORA: It *is* true. I have loved you more than anything in the world.

HELMER: You wretched creature— what have you done!

NORA: Let me go! You must not bear it for my sake. You must not take it on yourself.

HELMER: Enough melodrama.

>   *Locks with a key the door between the living room and the entry.*

You will stay here and give me a full account of yourself. Do you understand what you've done? Answer me! Do you understand?

>   *NORA looks at him fixedly.*

NORA: Yes, now I am beginning to.

HELMER *(pacing)*: What a horrific, rude awakening. For eight years— she— my joy and pride— a hypocrite, a liar— worse, worse, a criminal!— Oh, there's no bottom to this ugliness! Uh, uh!

> *NORA is silent and continues to look straight at him.*
>
> *He stops in front of her.*

I should have known. All your father's irresponsible traits— Shut up! All your father's irresponsible traits— you inherited. No religion, no morals, no sense of duty— oh, this is my punishment for being so easy on him. I did it for your sake and this is how you repay me!

NORA: Yes, this is how.

HELMER: You've destroyed all my happiness. You've ruined my future. Ah, this is too horrible to contemplate. I am in the clutches of an unscrupulous person. I am in his power—

He can do what he wants with me, demand anything of me— and I don't dare object. I am sinking down to the bottom— because of an irresponsible woman!

NORA: When I am gone, then you will be free.

HELMER: Enough. Your father had such expressions at the ready. How would it benefit me if you were "gone"? Not at all!

Krogstad can make *the thing* known, and if he does, people might think that I am behind it— that I encouraged you! Do you understand what you have done to me?

NORA *(with cold calm)*: Yes.

HELMER: This is so unbelievable— I cannot grasp— We must straighten this out. Take off the shawl. Take it off! I must appease him somehow. *The thing* must be hushed up at any price— As far as you and I are concerned, it must appear as it was before. But, of course, only in the eyes of the public. You will remain here in this house. You will not be permitted to bring up the children. I don't trust you with them—

Oh, to have to say this to you— you who I loved so dearly, and still—!

> *(Breaks off)*

Well, that's past. From now on it's no longer about happiness, it's about preserving what's left, the wreckage, the stumps, appearances—

> *There is a ring of the apartment door bell, out on the landing. HELMER starts.*

HELMER: What is it? So late. Would he—? Hide yourself, Nora! Say that you are sick.

> *NORA remains standing, immobile. HELMER goes over and unlocks the door to the entry.*

> *HELENE has answered the doorbell, opened the apartment door and been handed a letter by KROGSTAD.*

HELENE *(half undressed, in the entry)*: A letter came for the Mrs.

HELMER: Give it to me.[xc] Go back to bed.

> *Grasps the letter. HELENE exits.*

It's from him. I'll read it.

NORA: Read it.

> *He breaks the seal of the letter quickly; runs through a few lines; looks at an enclosed paper; a cry of joy.*

HELMER: Nora!

> *NORA looks questioningly at him.*

Nora!— Yes, yes, that's what it says. I am saved! Nora, I am saved!

NORA: And me?

HELMER: You too of course— we are saved. Both of us, both you and me. Look here. He sends back your promissory note. He says that he regrets and is sorry— a happy turn in his life— ah, it doesn't matter what he writes. We are saved, Nora!

> *Throws a glance at the promissory note, then tears the note and both letters in pieces, throws it all into the stove and watches while it burns.*

See there! It no longer exists— He wrote that ever since Christmas Eve you— Oh, these last three days must have been horrible for you.

NORA: Yes, I have fought a hard battle.

HELMER: And suffered agonies, not seeing any other way out than— No, we don't want to remember all this ugliness. We want to rejoice and repeat— it's over, it's over! But what is this— this stern look? Oh, I understand. You don't trust that I've forgiven you. But I have, I swear to you. I know what you did, you did out of love for me.

NORA: That's true.

HELMER: You have loved me as a wife should love her husband. You just didn't know how to judge the proper path. Do you think you are less dear to me because you don't understand how to act on your own? I wouldn't be a man if this feminine helplessness didn't make you doubly attractive. You must forget the harsh words I said when I thought the world was crashing down over me. I swear to you, I've forgiven you.

NORA: Thank you for your forgiveness.

> *NORA goes out through the door to the bedroom.*

HELMER: No, stay—

> *He looks in.*

HELMER (CONT'D): What are you doing in the alcove?

NORA *(inside)*: Throwing off my costume.

HELMER *(by the open door)*: Yes, do that. Settle down and calm your mind— regain your balance, my little scared songbird.

> *(Walks about in the vicinity of the door)*

Oh, how our home is soft and pretty, Nora. It's a nest for you, I have wide wings to cover you with. Tomorrow everything will look different. Soon everything will be back to normal. There is for a man something indescribably sweet and attractive in knowing in his heart that he has forgiven his wife. Don't worry yourself about anything, Nora— I will be both your will and your conscience— What's this? You've changed?

NORA *(entering in her everyday dress)*: Yes.

HELMER: But why, now, so late—?

NORA: I'm not sleeping tonight.

HELMER: But, Nora—

> *NORA looks at her watch.*

NORA: It's not so late. Sit down.

> *She seats herself at one side of the table with the doll on it.*
>
> *HELMER sits down at the table opposite her. He shoves the doll aside.*

HELMER: You're making me anxious, Nora. I don't understand you.

NORA: That's just it. You don't understand me. And I haven't understood you— until tonight. No, don't interrupt me. Listen to what I have to say— This is a settling of accounts.

HELMER: What do you mean by that?

NORA *(after a brief silence)*: Doesn't *one* thing strike you, about the way we are sitting here?

HELMER: What would that be?

NORA: We have been married for eight years. This is the first time that we two, husband and wife, are speaking together about serious things.

HELMER: Should I be constantly involving you in the concerns of a man's world, which you can't possibly help me with?

NORA: I'm not talking about that. I am saying, we have never sat seriously together, to try to get to the bottom of anything.

HELMER: But darling Nora, would you have wanted to?

NORA: That's just the point. You've never understood me— I have been wronged. First by Papa, then by you.

HELMER: What! By the two people who have loved you more than anyone else in the world!

NORA *(shakes her head)*: You never loved me. You only thought it was enjoyable to be in love with me.

HELMER: But Nora, what are you saying?

NORA: When I was in Papa's house he told me all his opinions, and so I had the same opinions— and if I had other ones, I hid them, because he wouldn't have liked that. He called me his doll child, and he played with me, like I played with my dolls. Then I came to your house—

HELMER: Is this how you're describing our marriage?

NORA *(undeterred)*: You arranged everything according to your taste, and so I acquired the same taste as you, or I just pretended to, I don't really know— I think it was both— first one and then the other. Now, when I look back at it, I think I have lived here like a beggar. I've supported myself by doing tricks for you. But you wanted it that way. You and Papa have committed a great sin against me. Nothing has become of me.

HELMER: Haven't you been happy here?

NORA: No, I've never been. I thought I was, but I've never been.

HELMER: Not— not happy!

NORA: No, only cheerful. You've always been so kind to me. But our home hasn't been anything other than a play house. Here I have been your doll wife, like at home I was Papa's doll child. And the children, in their turn, have been my dolls.

HELMER: There is some truth to what you're saying— however exaggerated and high-strung it may be. From now on it will be different. Playtime is over— now is the time for education.

NORA: Whose education? Mine or the children's?

HELMER: Both.

NORA: You are not the man to educate me on how to be a proper wife for you.

HELMER: You would—

NORA: And me— how am I prepared to educate the children?

HELMER: Nora!

NORA: Didn't you say you don't trust me with them.

HELMER: In the heat of the moment! How can you hold that against me?

NORA: It was very properly said. I don't have the power to undertake that task. There is something else I must do. I must educate myself. You're not the man to help me with that. I must do it alone. So, I am leaving you.

HELMER *(jumps up)*: What?

NORA: I must stand alone, if I am to understand myself and everything around me. I can't stay with you any longer.

HELMER: Nora, Nora!

NORA: I'll leave right away. Kristine will take me in for tonight, I think.

HELMER: You're out of your mind! You cannot! I forbid you!

NORA: You cannot forbid me anything now. I'll take only what belongs to me. I want nothing from you, now or later.

HELMER: This is insane!

NORA: Tomorrow I'll go home. It will be easier for me to find something there.

HELMER: Oh you blind, inexperienced creature!

NORA: I must get experience.

HELMER: Abandon your home, your husband and your children! Think of what people will say.

NORA: I can't.

HELMER: Oh, this is revolting. You can betray your holiest duties.

NORA: What are you counting as my holiest duties?

HELMER: The duties to your husband and your children!

NORA: I have other duties, equally holy.

HELMER: What?

NORA: Duties to myself.

HELMER: You are first and foremost a wife and mother.

NORA: I don't believe that any more. I believe I am first and foremost a human being— or in any case I will try to become one. I have to think these things through for myself.

HELMER: You're not clear about your position in your own home? You do have some feeling of morality?

NORA: Well, it's not easy to answer that. I don't know. I only know that my opinion is different from yours. I understand that laws are different from what I thought— but that those laws are just? I can't get that into my head. A woman doesn't have the right to spare her old dying father, or to save her husband's life.

HELMER: You speak like a child. You don't understand the society you're living in.

NORA: No, I don't. I want to get to know it— Then I'll see who's right, society or me.

HELMER: You're sick, Nora. You have a fever. I think you have lost your mind.

NORA: I have never felt as clear and certain as I do tonight.

HELMER: And clear and certain you abandon your husband and children?

NORA: Yes.

HELMER: There is only *one* possible explanation.

NORA: What?

HELMER: You don't love me anymore.

NORA: That is just it.

HELMER: Nora!

NORA: I no longer love you.

HELMER *(with hard-won composure)*: Is this also a clear and certain conviction?

NORA: Yes.

HELMER: Maybe you can enlighten me about how I lost your love?

NORA: It was tonight when the wonderful thing did not happen. It was then that I saw that you are not the man I had imagined you to be.

HELMER: Explain yourself— I don't understand.

NORA: When this came crashing in over me like a huge wave, I was absolutely certain. I thought— now comes the wonderful thing.

When Krogstad's letter lay out there it never entered my mind that you would give in to his demands. I was unshakably certain that you would say to him "make the thing known to the whole world." And when that had happened—

HELMER: Yes, what then? When I had given my own wife up to shame and dishonor—!

NORA: When that had happened, I was absolutely certain that you would step forward and say: "I am the guilty one."— That was the wonderful thing that I was hoping for and feared. And to prevent that, I planned to end my life.

HELMER: I would gladly work nights and days for you, Nora— bear grief and deprivation for your sake. But, no man sacrifices his honor for the one he loves.

NORA: A hundred thousand women have done just that.

HELMER: Oh, you think and speak like a foolish child.

NORA: Maybe. But you don't think or speak like the man I could be with. When your scare was over— not for what threatened me but for what might happen to you— it was as if nothing had happened. I was your little songbird, your doll, only now more delicate and frail.

>   *Stands up.*

In that moment it became clear to me that for eight years I've lived here with a stranger, and I had three children with him—

HELMER *(heavily)*: I see. I see. A chasm has opened up between us— Oh but Nora, couldn't we fill it back up?

NORA: As I am now, I am no wife for you.

HELMER: I have the power to become a different man.

NORA: Perhaps— if the doll is taken from you.

>   *NORA returns with her outerwear and a little carpet bag*
>   *which she puts on the chair next to the table.*

HELMER: Nora, Nora, not now! Wait till tomorrow.

> *She puts on her cloak.*

NORA: I can't stay overnight in a strange man's house.

HELMER: But couldn't we live here like brother and sister—?

> *She ties on her hat.*

NORA: You know very well it wouldn't be long—

> *She wraps her shawl around herself.*

Goodbye.

> *She sees the doll.*

I'll not see the little ones. I know they are in better hands than mine. The way I am now, I can't do anything for them.

HELMER: You are my wife.

NORA: When a wife leaves her husband's house, I've heard, according to the law, he is freed from all obligations to her. I free you from any obligation. There must be full freedom on both sides. Here have your ring back. Give me mine.

HELMER: This, too!

NORA: This, too.

HELMER: Here it is.

NORA: Good. Yes, so now it is over. Here are the keys. The maids can run the house, they know what to do better than I.

HELMER: Over, over! Nora, will you ever think about me?

NORA: I will often think of you and the children and this house.

HELMER: Can I write to you?

NORA: No— never.

HELMER: Oh, but to send you something, I must be allowed to—

NORA: Nothing, nothing.

HELMER: —help you, if you should need it.

NORA: No. I can't accept anything from strangers.

HELMER: Nora— can I never be more than a stranger to you?

> *She picks up her carpetbag.*

NORA: Then the most wonderful thing of all would have to happen.

HELMER: Name this most wonderful thing of all to me!

NORA: You and I would have to transform ourselves such that— I don't believe in anything wonderful anymore.

HELMER: But I want to believe in it. Name it! Transform ourselves such that—

NORA: That life together could become a true marriage. Goodbye.

> *She goes out through the entry.*

> *HELMER sinks down on a chair by the door and puts his hands over his face.*

HELMER: Nora! Nora!

> *He looks around and rises.*

She's no longer here.

> *A hope shoots up in him.*

The most wonderful thing of all—?!

> *From below we hear the sound of a heavy outer door slam shut. [See Appendix II.]*

Empty.

END OF PLAY

IBSEN'S ENDING:

HELMER sinks down on a chair by the door and puts his hands over his face.

HELMER: Nora! Nora!

He looks around and rises.

Empty. She is no longer here.

A hope shoots up in him.

The most wonderful thing of all—?!

From below we hear the sound of a heavy outer door slam shut.

END OF PLAY

NOTES

Note on the layout and this adaptation:

Ibsen assumes a proscenium stage. In *A Doll's House*, he describes a living room with four doors leading to four different spheres: the children's nursery, Torvald Helmer's private office, the couple's bedroom and dining room, and the hallway/entry leading to the apartment's front door. In addition, Ibsen demands that the entry, which is sometimes glimpsed through the living room door, in turn have four doors: the door into the living room; a door leading directly into Helmer's office; the front door of the apartment, equipped with mailbox and doorbell and leading to the staircase landing and the outside; and a door leading to the kitchen and servant area. He carefully describes the movement through all these doors and thus manipulates his characters to achieve the desired configurations that make up the dramatic action.

The Old Globe 2013 production took place in the 250-seat Sheryl and Harvey White Theatre, an intimate arena stage with two *vomitoria* and two staircases providing entrances to the acting area. This meant some modification of Ibsen's floor plan, reducing the entrances into the living room from four to three. In addition, none of these entrances had actual doors. Just as in Ibsen's script, the hallway was understood to have four doors, one leading directly to Helmer's office, one to the kitchen region, one leading to the living room, and one— the apartment door— to the stairs and the outside. But because of the offstage audible presence of the children, the entrance leading to the nursery sphere also connected to the kitchen and servants' quarters. In other words, the kitchen in the Old Globe production was imagined situated somewhere off stage between the entrance to the nursery region and the entrance leading to the entry and the outside. Ibsen's door leading to the couple's dining room and bedroom was cut and this sphere was entered via the entrance to the nursery, i.e., the nursery became "all private quarters" in the apartment, directly opposite the entrance from the entry and the outside.

While this script renders the dialogue of the Old Globe production as well as all stage business creating the children's presence, physically and psychologically, it does retain Ibsen's basic stage directions with regard to doors, entrances and exits, on the assumption that a given production, understanding the original directions, will solve any traffic problems its own way, just as the Old Globe production successfully reduced the living room's four entrances to three. Ibsen's directions "left" or "right"— applying only to a proscenium stage— have, however, been left out.

Note on the children's names:

Ibsen names the Helmer children Ivar, Bob, and Emmy. What in Ibsen's mind may have motivated the parents to give their firstborn the Norse name Ivar but the younger boy the British name Robert (Bob)— in Ibsen's complete draft it is Bobben ("the Bob"), even more of a petname— will be lost on a modern audience, who may instead wonder why the adapters Americanized the name. We chose to rename the boy Olaf, a reassuringly Norwegian name which does not call undue attention to itself.

Note on the text of the ending:

In the Old Globe production, the director chose to reverse the two last lines of the play, with the result that the very last note struck is one of dawning realization of finality, not of hope— however false— for the future. This script gives both endings. The choice is yours.

Note on intimate vs. polite address:

Where Ibsen's Dano-Norwegian, like so many other languages, distinguishes between the intimate and the polite form of address, modern English has only one form, the second person pronoun "you". Since social distance between speakers was strictly observed in Ibsen's world and maintained through forms of address, this script preserves Ibsen's careful drawing of lines by using lower case "y" for the intimate form, capital "Y" for the formal (Ibsen's *du*=you, Ibsen's *De*=You). As a rule, one could only use *du* addressing someone with whom one was on a first-name basis, i.e., a family member of equal status, an inferior (servant, child), or a very close friend. A wife might address her husband by his last name, and politely refer to him by his last name when speaking to someone with whom the husband was not on intimate terms. The use of first names was a privilege of intimacy. Torvald Helmer regrets having been close enough to Krogstad in their youth that they agreed to use first names and intimate address. As Ibsen uses shifts between first name address and polite address to reveal inner turmoil, inadvertent breaches of etiquette or deliberate overstepping of boundaries, the actors should be aware of the subtle signals embedded in the forms of address. Rank oversteps, slipping from "Mrs. Helmer" to "Nora" and then hastily changes back, Krogstad responds emotionally to Mrs. Linde's proposal by shifting from "Mrs. Linde" to "Kristine." Note that these emotional slips by the men are not accompanied by addressing the women *du*— that would have been going too far and would have implied agreement on the women's part. Note also that Mrs. Linde maintains her distance by not reciprocating with his first name "Nils"— though they have just agreed to (presumably) marry.

Final note on layout:

The layout of the apartment is crucial in the play's final moment: the Helmers live one flight up in a 19th century wooden apartment building. Consul Stenborg lives upstairs, presumably one flight above the Helmers. (The dancing at the Consul's is heard through the ceiling of the Helmers' living room.) Dr. Rank also lives in the house. His apartment is presumably on the first floor (he passes the Helmers on his way down from the party upstairs). If he visits the Helmers coming up from his own apartment or down from the upstairs, he would not wear an overcoat; when he comes directly from the outside without stepping into his own apartment first, he wears his fur coat, etc., but hangs it in the entry. If he is planning to go out with Helmer, he may bring his coat up to the Helmers' apartment to avoid having to stop by his own place on the way out, or, to warm it by the tiled stove, in the living room.

Each apartment opens via a lockable front door onto its respective landing of the common staircase. What we see in the Helmers' living room is the door between the living room and the entry. When that door is open, we can also see the apartment door leading onto the landing. This door has a mailbox on its inside, i.e., the mailman has access to the stairs and all the landings (the downstairs outer door may be open in the daytime or the mailman may have a key). This door also has a doorbell, normally answered by the Housemaid. The Helmers' entry has two more doors, one to Torvald Helmer's office and one to the kitchen. When Nora leaves the living room at the end of the play she first closes the living room door. We see that door closing. It may or may not make a noise as it closes. She then crosses the entry and goes through the apartment door out onto the landing, closing it behind her. This door is likewise not described as making a sound. But to indicate the finality of Nora's leaving, Ibsen then has her slam the downstairs *port*, the building's much heavier and bigger exterior door, as she steps from the house into the cold night outside. (The Norwegian has different words for the two types of doors, an inner door is a *dør*, a heavy outer one a *port*.) We hear that slam— "the door slam that reverberated around the world"— and it concludes the play as a non-verbal response to Helmer's last hopeful words. In order to preserve the finality of the play's last moment the audience must be able to visualize Nora walking down the stairs and interpret the door slam correctly. If the layout of the apartment is unclear to the audience, Ibsen's sequence of signs will not be effective. On the other hand, equivalent (i.e., equivalent to the door slam) signs of escape, hope, and finality can of course be found.

PROP LIST

Furniture Needs:

- Sideboard
- Sofa table
- Sofa/Settee
- Piano (upright)
- Tiled stove
- Fireplace tools (poker/broom)
- Central table with chairs
- Armchair

Hand Props:

- Packages, plain wrap
- Christmas tree
- Coin purse with coins and bills
- Bag of macaroons
- Children's outerwear, socks, scarves, etc. (Anne-Marie)
- Tablecloth
- Box of Christmas ornaments and tree decorations [including clip-on metal candle holders]
- Attaché briefcase (Krogstad)
- Briefcase/papers (Torvald)
- Embroidery (Nora)
- Promissory note
- Emmy's doll, destroyed

Hand Props (cont'd):

- Emmy's doll, repaired
- Ivar's saber
- Olaf's hobby horse
- Masquerade costumes (in a large cardboard box)
- Sheet music
- Oil/kerosene lamps
- Letter from Krogstad
- Letter in sealed envelope
- Nora's sewing basket
- Tambourine
- Pitcher of water and glasses
- Note to Krogstad
- Letter
- Knitting (Mrs. Linde)
- Cigar box
- Cigar
- Cigar cutter
- Ash tray
- Key chain
- Matches
- Hairpin
- 2 Visiting cards (Dr. Rank's)
- Letters (from mailbox)
- Krogstad's second letter
- Carpet bag

FOOTNOTES

i In *Et Dukkehjem* Ibsen describes the stage from the audience's point of view.

ii In Ibsen's proscenium layout, seen from the stage, the door USL leads, via the entry, to the landing and stairs and on to the outside world, while the door USR leads in to Torvald's private office, which is one of the rooms in the apartment. We later find out that Torvald's office has another door which opens directly into the entry (and from there to the outside), presumably for his business clients. (The apartment may have been planned for a doctor or other professional man in need of a separate room/office for consultations. Rank's apartment one floor below in the same building may have the same floor plan.)

iii This implies either that they are inherited from a wealthier home, probably Nora's childhood home, or purchased specifically in order to impress. Note also that the book cupboard in the living room is small.

iv Ibsen does not say that it is Christmas Eve, allowing the reader as well as theatregoer to find that out somewhat later.

v The apartment door— between the entry and the landing— has a lock, a mailbox, and a doorbell. Anyone visiting the Helmers would ring and be admitted and/or announced by the Housemaid. Nora appears not to have a key to this door since she rings the doorbell. (At this point she may have her arms too full of packages, preventing her from using the key. She may just want help to put the tree away.) In the last scene, she leaves her keys with Torvald.

vi The word used does not indicate overcoat; rather the kind of long or shawl-like cape that would fit over a dress with a slight bustle.

vii Note that the Porter does not enter the room, stops in the entry to deliver the tree and be paid. Ibsen clearly intends the door leading to the entry to be big enough so that when it is open one can see what is happening in the entry. In the premiere production the door to the entry as well as the door leading into Torvald's office were double doors.

viii Relatively new addition to Christmas in Norway, introduced at mid-century and becoming popular in the 1870s. It is not the first time the Helmers have had a tree— the decorations are all set to be put up and are treated as familiar objects— but there may still be a sense of excitement around this purchase, as well as anticipation of the fun when it is revealed to the children.

ix Norwegian currency from 1875 on was the *krone*, crown (replacing the old *speciedaler*; 1 *speciedaler*=4 *kroner*). One *krone*=100 *øre*. In the 1870s, a male laborer might expect to earn 2 *kroner* a day. A female seamstress might make 10-12 *kroner* a week.

x The point of the exchange is not the cost of Christmas trees but Nora's unusual generosity/extravagance. The Porter may expect a little extra but certainly not a 100% tip. The point can also be made if the Porter asks for a half crown instead of 50 *øre* and Nora pays him a whole crown.

xi The Norwegian *lukke* can mean either close/shut or lock. The matter of what doors are locked or merely closed is carefully thought out by Ibsen. The apartment door leading to the landing and the staircase serving all the floors is normally locked. The door to the entry can be locked— and is, later on— but at this point it would make little sense for Nora to lock it. We later find out that the door leading to Torvald's office can be latched on the living room side. The other doors that we see, the one to the nursery and the one leading to the dining room and the bedroom(s), are not locked in the play. We understand that the entry has a door leading directly to the kitchen, which in turn connects to the adjoining dining room. The staircase ends downstairs in a heavy exterior door, which is kept locked at night. At the back of the house, a smaller staircase serves the kitchen areas in all the apartments.

xii The purchases are wrapped in plain brown paper or paper sacks. They are not wrapped like American Christmas presents, boxed with ribbons and fancy paper. Nora takes out her purchases to admire them and show them to Torvald. Later that evening (Christmas Eve) they would simply be placed under the tree, unwrapped, to be "discovered" there.

xiii Both larks and squirrels were sometimes kept as caged pets.

xiv It was standard practice to pay servants part of their annual salary in kind, usually in the form of clothing material or articles of clothing. This was usually given as a Christmas bonus. Anne-Marie should have more than a standard bonus, but the Helmers are still in "economy" mode.

xv Nora and later Torvald use the interjection *ack*, "alas" but as it has a light feel and should be one syllable, it is simply rendered "aah."

xvi Nora refers to her father as *pappa*, "Papa;" Torvald always uses the word "father." The Helmers' children use the words *pappa* and *mamma*. We have chosen to let Nora refer to her father as "Papa" but keeping the Norwegian *mamma* and *pappa* for the children's words for Nora and Torvald. The French-accented "papa" and "mama" sound too refined for the children.

xvii Here Ibsen introduces Nora's word *"vidunderlig"* which recurs with increasingly complex associations throughout the play. It is important that the word remain the same; both for the sake of the repetition, but also because Nora's vocabulary is understandably limited. Of the possible English options, we chose "wonderful" as the most flexible and Nora-ish.

xviii Subverbal exclamation of discomfort, minor disgust.

xix Torvald just introduced the word *kedelig* "boring" into the discussion. Nora uses the word several times in the play (another one of her favorite words), but with other overtones. Here Nora is both expecting something tiresome and annoyed at being interrupted. We chose "annoying," which fits the moment better.

xx Kristine addresses Nora with the intimate *"du"* (instead of the formal *"De"*), here indicated by spelling "you" with a lower case "y." (See **Notes**.) They were friends in school, hence the intimate address, although since that time circumstances have separated them socially and economically.

xxi Though they apparently went to the same school, they were never classmates; Linde is older than Nora (appx. 4 years older, if Nora married 8 years ago at 18 and Linde was forced to marry 10 years ago at 20 after the broken engagement to Krogstad). Linde treats Nora with some condescension.

xxii Most public travel was by coastal or fjord steamer. Some towns did not yet have railroads (cf. *Pillars of Society*) and train travel was more expensive than steamer. Linde has probably come from up north along the coast or from the eastern mountainous region. It cannot have been too far away, as Nora read in the local papers about Linde's husband's death.

xxiii *Aktiebanken*, the Stock Bank. A "stock bank" was a new type of business bank, based on shareholders' investments, not on deposited savings This type of bank contributed considerably to the country's growth and modernization. In 1880 there were 18 stock banks in Norway and 311 savings banks. With no tangible securities guaranteeing the money, this bank was much more vulnerable to market fluctuations, presumably with higher risk and higher yield, and depending on the good name of everyone involved, banker as well as clients. The personality and integrity of the Director of a stock bank was crucial to the success of the bank, as his word and reputation reassured the clients of the soundness of their investments. Torvald Helmer was presumably hired because of his reputation as an upright lawyer who never had anything to do with shady cases. His reputation and integrity are absolute conditions for the success of his bank, which explains his attitude toward living on credit, his intense dislike of Krogstad's familiarity, and his concern for his own reputation and good name.

xxiv/xxiv As expanded on later in the play, Torvald the aesthete does not approve of some female handcraft. He considers any utilitarian handcraft (sewing clothes, knitting) unattractive, while graceful crafts that result in decorative items (embroidery) are approved. The less useful, the better. (Crocheting can fit into either category, so may— although not a graceful activity— be approved by Torvald.)

xxv Women's options were limited: lower class women could be maids/servants, seamstresses, or factory workers; middle class women, office workers or shop clerks; upper class women, teachers or telegraph operators. Linde is solidly middle class. (Almost half of all working women in Norway were maids/servants.) What Nora might be qualified to do to support herself is unclear.

xxvi The Norwegian here has "*skilling*," the old smaller denomination mentioned in the proverbial expression. Idiomatically "not a penny" works, as the point is "not a whit" and not any exact amount.

xxvii In 1845 unmarried women from 25 on had the same limited legal rights as men 18-25. Married women had no rights. In 1869 both men and women came of age at 21, but married women were still ruled by their husbands. In 1888 married women acquired some legal rights, though the husband still controlled the joint property (their home).

xxviii First appearance of another of Nora's favorite words, *uhyre* (rendered throughout as "tremendous").

xxix An indication of the Helmers' social life, at the point of being catapulted from struggling middle class couple with aspirations to important players in their community. So far it seems Nora's only company has been Torvald and Dr. Rank. She makes the point that Torvald has not liked her having other friends.

xxx Respectful address using title only.

xxxi Indicates exterior stairs or internal stairs between floors.

xxxii Rank is showing some, perhaps involuntary, professional curiosity disguised as raillery. The word choice is unfortunate and almost insulting; it probably reflects his preoccupation with his own deterioration or "rotting."

xxxiii Another recurring word in Nora's basic vocabulary, *umådelig* ("enormous").

xxxiv Medium-strong oath, swearing by Christ's *død og pine*, "death and suffering." The closest in vocal impact may be "hell and damnation." We upped it to "God damn it to hell" for equivalent shock value.

xxxv Nora is directing the remark to Torvald, asking his permission to present Mrs. Linde to him.

xxxvi Telegram from whom to whom? To the place where Linde has been living till now? Why? This is clearly a fib of Nora's to back up her invented story.

xxxvii Winter coat for men or women of means; may also signify someone of frail constitution needing extra warmth in the winter. Nora later admonishes Rank to stay warm. The fact that he warms his furcoat by the stove is another indication that his health is delicate.

xxxviii A sign of gracious acceptance of Mrs. Linde by Torvald Helmer, agreeing to be seen together with Rank in her company. She must be absolutely respectable, both in behavior and looks, to warrant Torvald's suggestion.

---

xxxix Is this a new idea for Krogstad? It is likely that he had thought of calling in the whole loan as one way to force Nora, another way being to reveal the forgery he strongly suspects. To Nora, just telling Torvald about the loan would be horrible, as her next line reveals.

xl In Act I, Helene was asked to place the tree in the middle of the room, creating circular movement around the tree and giving it absolute focus. In Act II it has served its purpose and been pushed into a corner. The tree could be on either side of the piano here, obviously so close that it does not obstruct the traffic through either of the two flanking doors. (In the Old Globe production it was first shown with burnt down candles, then removed.)

xli In Act II, both the new placement (pushed into a corner) and the appearance of the tree indicate that it has served its purpose. The purpose of the tree was to provide the family an extended magic moment of candlelight beauty and awe— note that Christmas trees were often decorated behind closed doors, so that the full effect of the lit tree would hit the family when the (often double) doors were flung open. Very theatrical. Modern audiences also tend to forget that the lit tree was an ephemeral and special thing, lasting only as long as the short burning candles lasted. Audiences used to Christmas trees with electric lights turned on for weeks tend to overlook this fact. Sometimes, the decorations would not be disturbed until the very last tree event of the season, the "dancing the tree out of the house" or "the plundering of the tree," so that the tree magic could be repeated for the family on one or more other occasions during the holiday season by replacing the burnt-out candles with new ones. But on Christmas Day, the Helmers' tree has already been "plundered," i.e., at least some of the edible treats appear to have been eaten (which cannot be done without destroying the decorations). Ibsen visually underscores the cataclysmic and final nature of the previous evening by suggesting that this year the magic event is unrepeatable or not to be repeated.

xlii The day was the most important holiday of the year, traditionally reserved for church going and the family. Visiting was discouraged, even by close neighbors.

xliii The box could contain more than one outfit of Nora's, possibly also Helmer's domino that figures in the action later.

xliv The 3rd person direct address using someone's title is very respectful; the use of the first name indicates intimacy. Anne-Marie is the only character in this play who would address Nora specifically this way.

xlv Implied cause/effect: Anne-Marie was good to little Nora because Nora did not have any other mother. Children need mothering, any mother will do, the mothering instinct bids a woman to mother anything needing it. Cf. Mrs. Linde mothering Krogstad's motherless children.

xlvi The word "ball" inflates the event in her imagination. Nora may be the only dancer at the party. The layout of the Stenborgs' apartment would not include a ballroom. The word was probably introduced into the conversation about this particular party by the term "costume/masquerade ball."

xlvii A consul was a man of consequence. In 1877, Norway had 210 persons in various levels of consular positions. There were 11 consuls general (the most prestigious) and 33 regular consuls. Stenborg is one of the 33.

xlviii Famous Italian folkdance in 3/8 or 6/8 time. The form Nora has learnt is the increasingly provocative solo dance. The premiere production in Copenhagen in December 1879 used Henrik Rung's music for the play *Gioacchino* while the subsequent production in Christiania used Holger Simon's composition from Bournonville's ballet *Napoli*. Mme de Staël's novel *Corinne* connects the tarantella with Italian joy of life, as contrasted with British formality. Some scholars have connected Nora's tarantella with existential tragedy, others with masquerade and role-playing, yet others with general theatricality.

xlix Ibsen refers to *tabes dorsalis*, the advanced form of syphilis of the spine, also euphemism for general syphilis.

l Rank lives downstairs in the same building, and his apartment may have a layout similar to the Helmers', allowing Rank a separate office for seeing patients. (Until recently he has apparently had patients, and his tendency to "diagnose" is clear with regard to both Linde and Nora.)

li Linde may be overstating the fact for effect here; she is probably no more than 3-4 years older, relating to Nora like an older sister.

lii Elsewhere we hear that Torvald does not like knitting. The only needlework he approves of is embroidery, emblematic of his whole attitude to women.

liii The intricate rules for polite address are touched on in **Notes**. This is the passage where Ibsen refers to the practise of becoming intimate friends by mutually agreeing to use first names. Common courtesy required that you could only say *"du"* to someone with whom you were on a first-name basis, which was generally restricted to members of your close family. People outside the family were politely referred to with their title, with or without the last name, and addressed *"De."* Etiquette also required that when A talked to intimate friend B referring to A's intimate friend C, with whom B was not intimate, A should refer to C by C's last name. For example, Nora refers to her husband as "Torvald" both when speaking to Mrs. Linde and Dr. Rank, breaching etiquette with Mrs. Linde but correctly with Rank. In business contexts it was possible for A and B to address each other informally, but as soon as another person was present who was not an intimate friend, A and B had to address each other formally.

liv Torvald has a point. Krogstad's breach of etiquette (cf. note liii) was unacceptable. The suggestion of intimacy, past or present, between Krogstad and Torvald would indeed compromise Torvald and undermine his position at the bank. Given the type of bank (Stock Bank) he is to head up, his personal reputation and integrity are unquestionable requirements. He is more a guarantor of above-board dealings than an administrator. To suggest to a modern audience the extent of his transgression, Torvald quotes Krogstad as addressing him "Torvald, Torvald" instead of "you, you Helmer."

lv Nora thought for a moment that Rank had found out something about her own situation with Krogstad, which is uppermost in her mind.

lvi The expression he uses is Biblical (Matthew 24:15 and 1 Macc. 1:57), referring to the "abomination of desolation."

lvii Possibly Biblical overtone here, cf. "visiting the iniquity of the fathers upon the children unto the 3rd and 4th generation" (2 Mos. 20:5).

lviii The force of her refusal to join Rank in his line of thought derails him and both go on with banter, which also shows that they have talked about Rank's inherited disease before. This is not new information, more a shared ritual.

lix It was believed that syphilis could be transmitted from father to son (cf. Ghosts).

lx The Norwegian fruentimmer implies mild condescension and dismissal on Rank's part. Overtones of the word "female" are here "middleclass busybody," "older woman," "dowd," "limited human being," "hen."

lxi The name of the color ("flesh colored") was considered too risqué and was left out of the play at the 1879 premiere.

lxii Alludes to John 15:13: "Greater love hath no man than this, that a man lay down his life for his friends."

lxiii An enormous breach of etiquette; Rank has never addressed Nora by her first name before. Very intimate.

lxiv Rank catches himself and reverts to the previous formal distance between them. Note that although he called her "Nora" he never changed from the formal "You" to "you."

lxv Apprehension, fear of something bad about to happen, pointing toward the future, not just "something wrong" in the moment. Could be the very first inkling Rank has of Nora's distress, interpreting various signs to point at pregnancy. His concern is discreet and appears to stem from real care for Nora.

lxvi Profession used as title; common polite practice in order to sort men into categories and assign relative worth.

lxvii Krogstad is dressed for travel into the country for a day or so. Do we see him differently dressed when he comes to visit Kristine later? Ibsen does not say, assuming Krogstad to have resumed urban gear.

lxviii Again possible religious overtone, as previously.

lxix Nora does not sit down to play (she may not be a good pianist), also it would take too long. She only wants to stop Torvald from going to the mail box. Note that in the original she beats the first few measures, either banging them out on the piano or simply beating the rhythm— if the latter, probably also humming the tune.

lxx Rank is a medical man, an observer, draws conclusions from signs, symptoms. He is also more sensitive to Nora's moods than Torvald and senses her underlying desperation and how close she may be to hysteria. His comment can also be medical advice about a woman who is pregnant. Rank later wonders whether Nora is pregnant and therefore so unpredictable and unruly. Both men are dealing with her as an object, Torvald very condescendingly ("the child"), Rank less so.

lxxi Torvald has told Rank about Nora's fear of failure at the party, her fear of Krogstad; Rank has told Torvald about Nora's supposed surprise second costume. In other words, the men continually freely share information about Nora and betray her confidences.

lxxii Probably a watch brooch; wrist watches were rare.

lxxiii Mrs. Linde and Krogstad are not intimate and use the formal *"De"* (You) throughout, although in the course of this scene they decide to join their lives. The breakthrough is indicated by Krogstad addressing Linde by her first name "Kristine."

lxxiv Krogstad takes a risk and uses Mrs. Linde's first name.

lxxv Linde readily agrees to Krogstad's suggestion, hiding her joy behind a sensible and understandable response. A respectable woman did not walk the streets alone at night.

lxxvi A domino is a black formal hooded cape that serves as a masquerade wrap— then usually accessorized with a half mask. There is no indication Torvald was otherwise dressed in anything but standard formal evening wear to the Consul's party: black coat with black or white waistcoat, white shirt and ribbon, worn at formal occasions, dinner parties, concerts, etc.

lxxvii A large room, but cannot be too large if the apartment floorplan is like the Helmers'.

lxxviii The sequence with Mrs. Linde about knitting reflects Torvald's opinions and his idolization of the female (who should be seen in beautiful pursuits), but he would not have said all this if he were sober. He knows this himself when he immediately comments on the champagne. We later find out that both Torvald and Rank had drunk a great deal of champagne at the Stenborgs. The infamous comment by Torvald that knitting looks "Chinese" was cut and replaced by exaggerated knitting motions.

lxxix Torvald really should accompany her home; he is not behaving correctly.

lxxx She probably noticed his "liveliness" as she was dancing the tarantella for him and knew the precarious state of his health.

lxxxi *Doctor Medicinae,* the academic title of someone with a doctorate in medicine. In 1874 only five medical doctors in Norway had earned the doctorate. Rank is a rare medical man, probably a researcher as well as a practitioner.

lxxxii Biblical tone in the original, echoing "The Lord will pass over that door" (2 Mos. 12: 23). Rank is on his way from the party upstairs down to his own apartment, does not wear an overcoat. In the following scene, the levels of formality are carefully observed: Torvald and Rank address each other as "du" ("you") as do Torvald and Nora, while Nora and Rank use "*De*" ("You") consistently.

lxxxiii The kind of match which can be struck against any surface. Where does Nora strike it? Shoe sole? May show ankle and more— she is wearing the tarantella costume.

lxxxiv The Norwegian "*farvel*" is more colloquial and more often used than "Goodbye" in English. The feeling when Rank leaves is more like "see you later," the double meaning of his parting words is subtler in the original. The whole exhange between Nora and Rank is quite light; Torvald does not pick up on any significant overtones. If the subtext is stressed in performance, Torvald looks like an idiot when he does not understand anything.

lxxxv Implies the household has at least one more young maid aside from the housemaid Helene. As she is preparing to leave, Nora later refers to the maids when she says they know how to run the household better than she. On the other hand, Mrs. Linde tells Krogstad that it is safe to talk at the Helmers' as the maid is asleep. It is unclear how many maids the Helmers have. It is possible that only one (Helene) is a live-in maid, the others employed for specific daytime duties. Anne-Marie is not included among the maids; her position as nanny and mother substitute has more status.

lxxxvi Torvald addresses and refers to Rank as simply "Rank," while Nora consistently calls him "Dr. Rank." The easy camaraderie of last name address is a male province. Nora would not dream of addressing or referring to Mrs. Linde as simply "Linde."

lxxxvii Rank refers to the decomposition of the corporal body also in his earlier scene with Nora when he comments on Torvald's delicacy and idealism— obviously a carefully cultivated pose that has completely convinced Nora and Rank. (Nora tells Kristine that Torvald cannot stand seeing women knitting or sewing, he can only tolerate seeing them embroidering. Rank, knowing how much Torvald hates death and bodily functions, tells Nora he will refuse to admit Torvald once he has taken to his sick bed. Torvald finds borrowing money ugly— and he is a bank manager!— and so on.)

lxxxviii See note lxxvi above.

lxxxix Extremely chopped up speech, unformed sentences, Nora can't find the words. As she later explains, she is on one hand prepared to do what she feels to be the heroic thing— suicide— but on the other she is expecting "the wonderful thing," namely that Torvald will prevent her from committing suicide and take the blame on himself. Her impulse here must be two extremes— take off or stay. The dash for the door— one impulse taking over temporarily? Cowardice, instinctive flight?

xc Torvald exercises the legal right of a husband to read mail addressed to his wife.

ABOUT THE AUTHORS

Henrik Johan Ibsen was born on March 20, 1828, in Skien, a small lumbering town of southern Norway. At just age 15, escaping his father's financial misfortune, Henrik moved to Grimstad, a hamlet of some 800 persons 70 miles (110 km) down the coast. There he supported himself as an apothecary's apprentice while studying nights for admission to the university, using his few leisure moments to write Catilina (1850), his first play. In 1862, he exiled himself to Italy, where he wrote the tragedy Brand, a semi-dramatic poem about a zealous priest. He moved to Germany in 1868, where he wrote one of his most famous works: A Doll's House, which follows protagonist Nora and her husband Torvald as she discovers her true self and realizes how far her life with Torvald has lead her off her own path. By 1891 Ibsen had returned to Norway a literary hero. He died on May 23, 1906 in Oslo, Norway.

Anne-Charlotte Hanes Harvey is a Swedish-born translator/dramaturg/playwright who specializes in the language and plays of Ibsen and Strindberg. Her unique platform translations have served a wide range of productions, from academic, to regional theatre, to Broadway, including adaptations by David Chambers, Jon Robin Baitz, Christopher Shinn, Kirsten Brandt, Mabou Mines, and others. Committed to providing global access to these works, she provided source texts for local language productions in Mysore, India and Beijing. She has translated/dramaturged seventeen plays by Strindberg as well as TYA plays by experimental Unga Klara and the Puppet Theatre TITTUT. Ibsen productions include Ghosts (Old Globe; North Coast Rep), Hedda Gabler (South Coast Rep; Broadway 2001 and 2009; North Coast Rep), Intimate Ibsen (ion), and A Doll's House (Old Globe; Raven Theatre 2020). She is the author of Fade to White and Dinner With Marlene. She is Professor Emerita of Theatre at San Diego State University.

Kirsten Brandt is an award-winning playwright, director, and producer. She served for six seasons as Artistic Director of Sledgehammer Theatre where she directed over a dozen plays and wrote Berzerkergäng, The Frankenstein Project, and NU. She was Associate Artistic Director of San Jose Repertory Theatre, where she directed over half a dozen plays and co-wrote the musical The Snow Queen. As a director, her work has been seen at The Old Globe, TheatreWorks, La Jolla Playhouse, Utah Shakespeare, Marin Theatre Company, San Diego Repertory, Santa Cruz Shakespeare, North Coast Repertory, and Arizona Theatre Company. She is the co-adapter of Henrik Ibsen's A Doll's House. Her other plays include Coded, The Mechanic's Daughter, The Waves, an adaptation of Wuthering Heights, as well as the telematic, multi-site play The Thinning Veil and the site-specific The Open Door. She is an Assistant Professor at San Jose State University. www.kirstenbrandt.com

ABOUT STAGE RIGHTS

Based in Los Angeles and founded in 2000, Stage Rights is one of the foremost independent theatrical publishers in the United States, providing stage performance rights for a wide range of plays and musicals to theater companies, schools, and other producing organizations across the country and internationally. As a licensing agent, Stage Rights is committed to providing each producer the tools they need for financial and artistic success. Stage Rights is dedicated to the future of live theatre, offering special programs that champion new theatrical works.

To view all of our current plays and musicals, visit:

www.stagerights.com

Made in the USA
Middletown, DE
08 August 2023

36319893R00050